Rainer Maria Rilke

(4 December 1875–29 December 1926)

Rainer Maria Rilke
Aspects of his Mind and Poetry

Edited by William Rose
and G. Craig Houston

With an Introduction
by
Stefan Zweig

GORDIAN PRESS
New York
1970

First Published 1938

Reprinted 1970, by Gordian Press Inc.
By arrangement with
Sidgwick & Jackson, Ltd.

Library of Congress Catalog Card Number – 73-114098
SBN 87752-092-5

CONTENTS

INTRODUCTION

By STEFAN ZWEIG

INTRODUCTION

A VOLUME of essays on the beloved poet Rainer Maria Rilke by scholars who have made a special study of his work may seem to need no introduction. But perhaps I have a certain right to speak—a right which is also a precious and painful privilege, for I am one of the very few in this country who knew him personally, and a poet can never be fully understood in all his aspects unless one has in mind a portrait of the *man*. So just as one likes to preface a book with a portrait of the author, perhaps I may be allowed to try to present a silhouette of the poet I knew.

In our age a true poet is rare. Even more rare perhaps is a genuinely poetic existence, a perfect way of life, and whoever has had the good fortune to witness such matchless harmony of life and creative activity may not evade the duty of bearing testimony to this spiritual miracle for the benefit of his generation and perhaps of posterity. For many years I had the opportunity of meeting Rainer Maria Rilke frequently. We had long conversations in numerous cities, I have preserved the letters which he wrote to me, and he made me the precious gift of the manuscript of his famous story, *Die Weise von Liebe und Tod des Cornets Christoph Rilke*. Yet I would not dare to say that I was his friend, at least in the more intimate sense of the term, for the great respect I felt for him always put a certain distance between us. Rilke seldom conferred upon anyone the favour of his intimate friendship, and you can see from his letters that in thirty years he only addressed a correspondent as " friend " perhaps two or three times. Even this was deeply characteristic of him. He was extremely shy of revealing, in words or in any other way, what he felt. He liked to remain unobtrusively in the background and was reticent about his personal circumstances. In fact, when I try to call to mind the various people I have met in the course of my life, I can remember none who succeeded in remaining personally so inconspicuous as Rilke.

There are poets who, as a defence against the importunity of the world, create for themselves a mask of haughtiness and hardness. There are others who, for the sake of their work, take refuge in their poetry and, holding completely aloof, are inaccessible to their fellow-men. This was not the case with Rilke. He came into contact with

a large number of people, he travelled in many
countries, but his defence was his complete modesty,
an indescribable quietness and gentleness that
enveloped him in an inviolable aura.   In a railway
carriage, in a restaurant, at a concert he would
never have attracted attention. He wore the
simplest clothes, though they were always neat
and in good taste, avoiding any adjunct that might
have emphasised the fact that he was a poet.   He
refused to allow his photograph to appear in
newspapers or periodicals.   With inflexible resolution he preserved his privacy and did not stand out
among other men, for he desired to observe and
not to let himself be observed.

Picture to yourselves a room in Munich or
Vienna, where a dozen or twenty people are
sitting together engaged in conversation.   A
delicate, youthful-looking man enters, and the
others do not even notice him as he comes through
the door. This again is characteristic. Quietly,
with a light tread and short steps, he is suddenly
among them, has shaken hands with one or two
acquaintances, and is now sitting with slightly
bent head so that his eyes, those wonderfully light
and animated eyes which alone reveal his soul,
cannot be seen. He sits quietly, his hands lying
folded on his knees, and listens—and I have never

encountered a better, a more sympathetic listener. He is completely absorbed in what is being said, and when he himself speaks it is so softly that one hardly realises how beautiful and mellow his voice is. He is never impetuous, never tries to persuade or convince his hearers, and when he feels that too many people are listening to him, that he has become the focus of attention, he soon withdraws again into himself. Real conversation, such as one remembers all one's life, was only possible when alone with him, and the most favourable time was the evening, when the room was shadowed in twilight, or while walking with him in the streets of a foreign city.

Rilke's reserve, however, had in it nothing of haughtiness or apprehension, and it would be utterly false to think of him as a neurotic, a warped personality. He could be quite unconstrained and talk in the most natural way, and I have more than once seen him in high spirits. Anything strident or coarse, however, was intolerable to him. He found a noisy person agonising and any importunate pestering by admirers was mirrored in the timid, startled expression that came into his face. Yet it was wonderful to see how his gentle manner had the power of keeping even the most tenacious of these persecutors at a distance, quelling the noisiest and reducing the most self-confident to diffidence. His presence always seemed to clear the atmosphere. I believe that no one ever ventured to utter an obscene or coarse word in front of him, and that no one had the courage to retail literary gossip or spiteful scandal to him. Like oil poured on stormy waters he created a circle of calm round him wherever he went. It was amazing to see his power of radiating tranquillity, subduing any jarring element and resolving discord into harmony.

Just as he set the tone in any company where he was present, he also impressed his personality on every room in which he dwelt. As he was poor he usually lived in mean lodgings, one or two rented rooms containing commonplace furniture; but just as Fra Angelico was able to transform his drab cell into a place of beauty, so Rilke was able to invest his surroundings with his own personal quality. The things he added were always trifles— a flower in a vase on his desk, a reproduction or two that he had purchased for a few shillings on his walls—for he neither liked nor wanted luxury. But he knew how to arrange these things with an eye to symmetry so that the whole room at once presented an ordered unity. By this inner discernment he neutralised any conflicting element.

It was not essential for his surroundings to be beautiful or costly, but they had to be harmonious. With his genius for form he could not endure even in his outward life anything formless, chaotic, fortuitous or slovenly. When he wrote a letter in his beautiful round, upright hand, he would allow neither correction nor blot to mar it. If his pen slipped he would ruthlessly tear up the letter and begin it again. When he returned a borrowed book it came back carefully wrapped in tissue paper, tied with a coloured string, and accompanied by a flower or a few lines of thanks. When he went on a journey the packing of his trunk was a work of art.

In this way he set his mark inconspicuously but definitely on everything he did. Just as the Hindus have their saints on the one hand and the untouchables, whose sleeve no one dares to brush, on the other, so it was essential to Rilke that he should encircle himself with a certain layer of aloofness. It was only a very thin layer behind which the warmth of his nature could be felt, yet it guarded impenetrably his unsullied essence as a fruit is protected by its husk. It shielded that which he considered to be the ultimate necessity for an artist—the freedom to live his life as he desired. No successful and prosperous poet or

artist of our own times has ever been so free as
Rilke, who allowed himself to be bound by no tie.
He had no regular habits and no address. He did
not really even have a fatherland, for he was as
much at home in Italy as he was in France or
Austria, and one never knew where he was. When
one met him it was almost invariably by chance.
In a Paris bookshop or a Viennese drawing-room
one would suddenly see his friendly smile and feel
the pressure of his soft hand. Then with equal
suddenness he would vanish, and we who loved
and honoured him did not ask where he was to
be found or call on him if we knew, but waited
until he came to us.

Yet each time that we of the younger generation
saw and spoke to him it brought us spiritual
refreshment and happiness. Try to imagine what
we younger writers learned from a great poet
whose human aspect did not disappoint, who was
not too busy to devote his time to us, who was
not concerned with the practical implications of
his work, who cared only for his poetry and nothing
for its effect, who never read critiques and never
allowed himself to be gaped at or interviewed, who
was always sympathetic and retained to his last
hour a wonderful interest in everything new.
For a whole evening I have heard him reading to

a circle of friends, not his own verses, but those of some young poet; and I have seen whole pages of excerpts from books copied out in his beautiful handwriting in order to give them to someone he thought might be interested. It was touching to see his humble veneration for a poet like Paul Valéry, to see him translating his poems and, at the age of fifty, speaking of a poet only five years his senior as of a master whose stature he could not hope to attain. He found happiness in admiration for others, and this was essential in the latter years of his life. You will forgive me if I do not describe to you how this man suffered from the War and the time which came after it, when the world was bloodthirsty, ugly, brutal, barbaric, and the quiet refuge that he tried to create round himself was shattered. I shall never forget his air of bewilderment when I saw him in uniform. He had to overcome years of spiritual paralysis before he could again write poetry, but when he did he produced the matchless perfection of the *Duineser Elegien*.

I have tried to indicate in brief outline something of the pure art of life practised by Rilke, who screened himself from the public eye, who never raised his voice among men, and whom one hardly seemed to hear breathing. Yet when he passed from our midst, there was no one whose loss was so deeply felt as was that of this gentle poet, and only now do Germany and the world realise that they have been bereft of something that is irretrievable. When a great poet dies it sometimes seems to his countrymen as if poetry had died with him. Perhaps England had a similar experience when within the space of half a decade it lost first Keats, then Shelley and Byron. In such tragic moments the dead poet appears to his contemporaries as a symbol of poetry itself, and they tremble lest he should be the last upon whom they will look. When we of the German tongue to-day utter the word 'poet' we think of Rilke, and only when we look round for his beloved presence in all the familiar places do we realise that it has passed from us to become a statue in the marble groves of immortality.

STEFAN ZWEIG

RILKE AS REVEALED IN HIS LETTERS

By G. CRAIG HOUSTON

RILKE AS REVEALED IN HIS LETTERS

VOLUMES of selected letters from the large body of Rilke's remarkable correspondence have been published, with almost yearly regularity, since the poet's death in December 1926, and I have thought to see emerging from these personal records such essential features of his mind and character as will allow of true portrayal. The picture will necessarily be incomplete, but it may serve, perhaps, until such time as all existing material is published in its integrity.

It must be acknowledged at the outset that the greatest difficulty encountered, in attempting this task, has been due not to the incompleteness, but rather to the almost overwhelming richness of the material which the published letters provide. The design of the editors—the poet's daughter and son-in-law—in making their selection of letters or parts of letters has been to give such material as will illustrate Rilke's own statement in his last will and testament, where he said that he had put into his letters a part of his creative genius.

This published material consists of *Briefe und*

Tagebücher aus der Frühzeit, 1899-1902 ; the thirteen
letters to the artist Oskar Zwintscher, who visited
Westerwede to paint the portraits of Rilke and his
wife in the first year of their married life ; *Briefe aus
den Jahren 1902-1906*, which are filled with the Rodin
experience and the record of the first years in Paris ;
Briefe aus den Jahren 1906-1907, written after the
break with Rodin, the large majority of which are
addressed to his wife; *Briefe aus den Jahren 1907-1914*,
when he was living in Paris, Italy and Germany,
or visiting Algiers, Egypt and Spain ; *Briefe an
einen jungen Dichter*, covering the period February
1903 to Christmas 1908 ; *Briefe an eine junge Frau*,
written between August 1919 and February 1924 ;
two characteristic *Briefe über Gott*, published
separately ; *Briefe an seinen Verleger, 1906-1926*,
which show us the author Rilke, writing in a
dignified and often markedly business-like tone ;
Briefe aus Muzot, 1921-1926, giving a record of his
last years which were spent in Switzerland ; the
French edition of the *Lettres à Rodin* from June
1902 to May 1913 ; further, such extracts from
letters to friends which appear only in their published recollections, more especially those quoted
by Maurice Betz in his recent volume *Rilke vivant*,
and the valuable selection from letters to Rilke's
Swiss friend, Frau Wunderly-Volkart, published in

Professor von Salis' book on *Rilkes Schweizer Jahre*; and, finally, the recently published letters of the war period, *Briefe aus den Jahren 1914-1921*. There are, in all, some twelve hundred published letters, forming but a part of those which have been preserved. In view of the nature of the editing, they necessarily tell us more about Rilke's mind and philosophy than about other aspects of his daily life. But, indeed, I believe this must be true of any letters Rilke ever wrote.

There is an old saying that the child is father to the man, and students of Rilke, in whatever light and from whatever angle they view him, are in full agreement as to its validity in his case. Divergence of opinion arises only when they seek to estimate and analyse the content of his childhood. Direct reference to it is rare in the published letters. But when it occurs, it is made deliberately and with a full sense of its implication. The most direct indictment of his school years, which we know to have been unhappy, will be found in a letter of 1920 to Generalmajor von Sedlakowitz. Unfortunately the great collection of Rilke's letters to his mother, in which we might reasonably expect to find most frequent mention of the details of his childhood, is not yet accessible. But Dr. Sieber, in his book on the poet's youth, has quoted a most significant phrase from one of these letters, a phrase which shows clearly Rilke's belief that the roots of his life's work went back to the experiences of his childhood.   It occurs in a letter which he wrote to his mother for Christmas 1923, not quite a year after the publication of the Sonnets and the Elegies. He vividly recalls the happiness of the Christmas festival at home ; how on Christmas Eve he and his mother would kneel together in prayer at the same prie-dieu, how his " beloved papa," as he calls him, would ring the bells, the sound of which seemed so festive and full of annunciation, and then how, finally, the doors would open and all the wonder of the Christmas tree be revealed. What remained with him vividly was not the memory of the gifts—they were long since forgotten—but the emotion aroused, the sensation of anticipatory joy, a feeling which returned to him even while he was writing his letter.   And he goes on to suggest that perhaps he has become a singer of joy because of this early training.   " Vielleicht bin ich deshalb, meine liebe Mama, ein solcher Rühmer der Freude geworden, weil Ihr mich zu so grosser Vorfreude erzogen habt."

The dominant note of his childhood, however, was not one of joyfulness. The character of his mother, undoubtedly remarkable but equally un-

lovable, was never congenial to the poet.   And
we can hardly be wrong in thinking that the atmosphere of fanatical religiosity which emanated from
her was, like the atmosphere of Edmund Gosse's
childhood, responsible in part for later spiritual
difficulties.

Many letters contain passages of indignant, even
bitingly ironic repudiation of Christian doctrine.
These can, perhaps, only be rightly understood in
the light of the religious associations of the poet's
childhood.   It is known, for example, that his
mother taught him to kiss in particular the marks
of the nails in the figure on the crucifix, as a means
of vivifying his sense of Christ's physical sufferings.
And although Rilke makes no reference to such
things later we are justified, from what we know
of his character, in believing that they must have
appeared to him, in his maturity, as an unwarrant-
able assault upon the susceptibilities of a highly
strung child.

Two aspects of his thought regarding Christianity are clearly evident in the letters.   He at all
times insists that adherence to the principles taught
by the founder of Christianity is the only solution
for the life of individuals and of nations ; he as
constantly objects to the doctrinal teaching of the
Church and, amongst the laity, to everything that

B

savours of a stereotyped conception.   We are left
with the impression that it was the sincerity of his
belief in the one which sharpened his criticism of
the other.   That it was the gloomier aspect of the
Catholic religion which predominated in his youthful associations is shown by a variety of passages
in the letters, as, for example, when he writes as a
student in Berlin to his friend Paula Becker at
Worpswede in November 1900, saying that the
first days of that month are for him always "katho-
lische Tage," because until he was sixteen or
seventeen he always spent the second of November,
All Souls, in graveyards, by the graves of strangers
or of his own people, graves which he could not
explain but which he brooded over in the lengthen-
ing winter evenings, and which first brought home
to him the idea that every hour is the hour of death
for some one.   The only grave he now visits at
this season, he adds, is the grave of Heinrich von
Kleist.

It would be a mistake, however, to deduce
from the many passages dealing with the solemni-
ties of life, which mark the correspondence from
beginning to end, that the writer was of a gloomy
or sorrowful temper.   Nothing could be further
from the truth.   There is a common tendency, of
which Rilke was well aware, to confuse the idea of

earnestness with that of melancholy.   He wrote a
specific warning against it.   The serious attitude
to life which is so manifest in all his writings has,
he says, nothing at all to do with melancholy.
For, in taking life seriously, he was only weighing
it with the true measures of weight ; he had
attempted to measure with the carat weight of the
heart in place of the false measures of suspicion,
happiness or luck.   This by no means implies a
refusal or rejection of any kind, but rather an
infinite and constantly renewed assent.   " Jenes
Schwer-nehmen des Lebens, von dem meine Bücher
erfüllt sind, ist ja keine Schwermütigkeit ... Jenes
Schwer-nehmen will ja nichts sein ... als ein
Nehmen nach dem wahren Gewicht, also ein Wahr-
nehmen ; ein Versuch die Dinge mit dem Karat
des Herzens zu wägen, statt von Verdacht, Glück
oder Zufall.   Keine Absage, nicht wahr ? keine
Absage ; oh, im Gegenteil, wieviel unendliche
Zustimmung und immer noch Zustimmung zum
Da-Sein ! "

And this assent, carrying with it the satisfaction
of a profound human instinct, is fundamentally
pleasurable.   From the days of his association with
Rodin this belief continued to increase.   He wrote
to his wife from Sweden in 1904 a description of
the poet-philosopher, Larsson, which is significant

in this connexion. The latter, he says, would
never be in danger of choosing an easy solution,
because he was wise enough to know that when
we accept the difficulty of life, it becomes easy
(since we have enormous resources of strength
within us), whereas to choose what is easy is an
act of infidelity, an evasion of life, a withdrawal
from the scene of action. " Er weiss, dass das
Schwere, indem wir es tragen, das Leichte ist (weil
wir im Grunde Riesenkräfte haben), dass aber das
Leichte tragen zu wollen eine Veruntreuung ist,
ein Sich-dem-Leben-Entziehen, ein Ausweichen vor
ihm."   And, in a letter to a young poet, he declares
epigrammatically that our concern is essentially
with what is difficult.   " Aber es ist Schweres,
was uns aufgetragen wurde, fast alles Ernste ist
schwer und alles ist ernst."   And we must adhere
to what is difficult, if we would make any claim
to having a part in life.   " Es ist aber klar, dass
wir uns an das Schwere halten müssen ; alles
Lebendige hält sich daran."   What we are to
understand by courage is a valiant attitude in
facing the strangest and most inexplicable things
that can happen to us.   " Das ist im Grunde der
einzige Mut, den man von uns verlangt : mutig
zu sein zu dem Seltsamsten, Wunderlichsten und
Unaufklärbarsten, das uns begegnen kann."   Irre-

parable wrong has been done to life because men have been cowardly in this sense. "Dass die Menschen in diesem Sinne feige waren, hat dem Leben unendlichen Schaden getan."

Although difficult, life was for Rilke something inviolably precious. He was able to write from Munich, on the 9th of October 1918, that not even the constantly increasing horror of the last years had been able to alter his belief in the fullness and goodness of existence. "Da bekenne ich denn, . . . dass ich das Leben für ein Ding von der unantastbarsten Köstlichkeit halte, und dass die Verknotung so vieler Verhängnisse und Entsetzlichkeiten, die Preisgebung so zahlloser Schicksale, alles, was uns diese letzten Jahre zu einem immer noch zunehmenden Schrecken unüberwindlich angewachsen ist, mich nicht irre machen kann an der Fülle und Güte und Zugeneigtheit des Daseins." It is his conviction that the valuable things of life come forth pure, unspoiled and fundamentally desirable from the midst of upheaval and destruction : " dass die Güter des Lebens rein und unverdorben und im Tiefsten begehrenswert aus Umsturz und Untergang hervorgehen." He wrote a short time before his thirty-first birthday, in 1906, that those who live with courage and resolution can never be deceived or disappointed in the

essential realities of life : " wer, wie Sie, so im
Grunde mutig und entschlossen und ernst zum
Leben steht, den kann es ja im Tiefsten und Wesentlichen nicht kränken und nicht enttäuschen : seine
Erwartungen und sein Wollen wirkt in der Richtung des Lebens, und es kann nicht anders, als
eins nach dem anderen weitertragen von Ziel zu
Ziel.   Nur, dass wir diese Ziele so wenig kennen
und erkennen, mag uns eine Weile verwirren ; im
Weitergehen werden wir doch immer einsehen und
zugeben, wie gut alles war."

Again and again, as he drew near the end of the
fifty-one years allotted to him as the span of life, he
expressed wonder at the beneficent ordering of his
experience, as, for example, when he wrote to his
friend and physician in 1912 : " Glauben Sie mir,
dass ich doch von nichts so ergriffen bin wie von
der unbegreiflichen, unerhörten Wunderbarkeit
meines Daseins, das von vornherein so unmöglich
angelegt war und von Rettung zu Rettung dennoch
fortschritt."   In truth, Rilke might well be considered as a living illustration of that theme which
is so characteristic of the German novel since
Goethe established it with his *Wilhelm Meister*—
the education of a character through life.   And the
letters might be regarded as the story of his education.   Perhaps, indeed, the only adequate treatment

would be an interpretation of them in this sense; but it must suffice here to say that the poet himself saw his life as a process of working towards the resolution of disharmonies. And since all his works are a confession, in that they mirror successively each stage of his progress, the main line of development could be traced out clearly in the writings of his various periods, however differentiated they may be by the artistic form or manner of each successive stage. He himself, in fact, suggests the outlines of such an analysis in an all-important letter to his Polish translator, in which he explains that the Elegies are the statement of his final assent to both life and death: " Lebens- *und* Todesbejahung." It is, indeed, a fascinating study to watch how the main themes of these great poems develop slowly, uninterruptedly, almost imperceptibly throughout the whole course of the correspondence.

I have emphasised the positive aspect of Rilke's outlook, because there has been a widespread tendency to see in his extremely sensitive poetry a shrinking from life, an attitude of mind which we commonly associate with our idea of the Austrian temperament, and which we rightly consider to have been convincingly exemplified in the great Austrian dramatist, Grillparzer. Closely linked with it is the conception of ' le malheur d'être poète.' In this connexion there is an illuminating passage in which Goethe's great poetic version of that theme, his drama *Tasso*—which made a very special appeal to Grillparzer—is summarily dismissed by Rilke as an unpleasant, ill-humoured book that falls far behind the significant facts of reality : " es ist ein missvergnügtes, übellauniges Buch ; das was historisch vor sich ging, war, glaub ich, bei weitem mehr, unbedingt müsste es noch einmal ganz anders geschrieben werden."

Rilke, no less than Goethe and Grillparzer, felt the vocation of poet to be difficult ; but *not* because it was, in its very nature, at variance with human living. Never could he have said with Grillparzer's Sappho :

> Dort oben war mein Platz, dort an den Wolken,
> hier ist kein Ort für mich, als nur das Grab.
>
> .   .   .   .   .   .
>
> Ein Biss nur in des Ruhmes goldne Frucht,
> Proserpinens Granatenkernen gleich,
> reiht dich auf ewig zu den stillen Schatten.

On the contrary, the poet revealed to us by the letters is one for whom art and human living are inseparably associated. A statement of his own, made rather less than a year before the completion of the Elegies, cannot be improved upon : " Viele haben sich durch Leichtnehmen des Lebens geholfen, indem sie ihm, so zu sagen, unter der Hand entrissen, was sie *doch* nötig hatten, oder sich seine Werte zu Räuschen machten, deren trübe Begeisterung sie dann rasch in die Kunst hinüberwarfen—; andre hatten keinen Ausweg, als die Abkehr vom Leben, die Askese, und *dieses* Mittel ist freilich um vieles reinlicher und wahrer, als jener gierige Betrug am Leben zugunsten der Kunst. Aber für mich kommt auch dieses nicht in Betracht. Da doch letzten Grundes meine Produktivität aus der unmittelbarsten Bewunderung des Lebens, aus dem täglichen unerschöpflichen Staunen vor ihm hervorgeht (wie wäre ich sonst zu ihr gekommen?), so sähe ich auch *darin* eine Lüge, sein mir Zuströmen irgendwann abzulehnen ; jede solche Versagung muss auch schliesslich innerhalb der Kunst selbst, mag sie potentiell noch so viel durch sie gewinnen, als Härte zum Ausdruck kommen und sich rächen : denn wer sollte auf einem so empfindlichen Gebiet ganz offen und zusagend sein, wenn er dem Leben gegenüber eine misstrauische, einschränkende und beängstigte Haltung hat ! " The suffering of life is a gain, since it brings to full strength the latent spiritual forces within us. Facing the horror of the War, he wrote on 17th September 1914:

" Wir überstehns. Und dann ists eine Gewalt
mehr in uns, und das Herz soll uns darüber mäch-
tiger geworden sein und alles Fühlbare heiliger
und reiner und verpflichtender." And about a
year later he wrote of Strindberg's *Dance of Death*
that, despite its terrible depiction of the desolation
of human life, it yet imparts a sense of the greatness of man, since he is able to face and depict this
desolation : " Erst nimmt sichs so heillos eigen-
sinnig aus, die Trostlosigkeit des Menschlichen
als sein eigentlich Absolutes darzustellen, aber
indem einer Macht hat auch noch über das Trost-
loseste, schwebt, unausgesprochen, ein Begriff
nicht abzugrenzender Menschengrösse über dem
Ganzen."

At another time he writes of his belief in work
and in the advantage of growing old : " Ich glaube
an das Alter, lieber Freund, Arbeiten und Altwerden,
das ist es, was das Leben von uns erwartet. Und
dann eines Tages *alt sein* und noch lange nicht
alles verstehen, nein, aber anfangen, aber lieben,
aber zusammenhangen mit Fernem und Unsag-
barem, bis in die Sterne hinein." As early as
the year 1899 he had declared : " meine Arbeit
[bleibt] die höchste Instanz und vor dem Blick
einer schenkenden Stunde [müssen] alle Eintags-
pflichten verstummen."

The claim of art upon his own life was something in the nature of a religious imperative. Writing in July 1921, when he knew that the great Elegies were already ripe within him, he said : " Wenn ich in mein Gewissen schaue, sehe ich nur ein Gesetz, unerbittlich befehlend : mich in mich selbst einschliessen und in einem Zug diese Aufgabe beenden, die mir im Zentrum meines Herzens diktiert wurde. Ich gehorche.—Denn Sie wissen es, hier wandelnd, habe ich nur das gewollt, und ich habe keinerlei Recht, die Richtung meines Willens zu ändern, bevor ich den Akt meiner Aufopferung und meines Gehorsams beendet habe."

This imperative was laid upon him from the beginning. He was conscious of it when he rejected his father's solicitous scheme that he should ensure his livelihood by adopting a profession and giving only his spare time to writing. It is the secret of the constant wandering and movement of his life. It dictated renunciation to him when, after the first visit to Worpswede on his return from Russia, he wrote from Berlin to Paula Becker that to think of a little house and home of his own would be an act of infidelity. " Verstehen Sie, dass es eine Untreue ist, wenn ich tue, als ob ich anderswo schon ganz erfüllt Herd und Heimat fände ? Ich darf noch kein Häuschen haben, darf

noch nicht wohnen. Wandern und Warten ist
meines." And when he married the young sculp-
tress, Clara Westhoff, and settled in the vicinity
of Worpswede, it allowed him little more than
a year and a half of happy married life before it
drove him on to Paris. His wife, sharing his
belief in the sacredness of vocation, was prepared
also to devote herself to art. He wrote a few
months later in explanation of their plans : "Ich
habe im vorigen Jahr einen kleinen Haushalt
gehabt mit meiner Frau zusammen (in einem
kleinen Dorfe bei Worpswede) ; aber der Haushalt
verzehrte zu viel, und so haben wir uns versprochen,
jeder als eingeschränkter Junggeselle, wie vorher,
der Arbeit zu leben. Das gibt auch jedem die
Möglichkeit, *dort* zu sein, wo es seine Arbeit
gerade braucht. Denn, da die Arbeit ganz obenan
stehen muss, sind wir auch bereit, eine örtliche
Trennung dann und wann auf uns zu nehmen, wenn
es notwendig ist. Wir haben viel Zeit verloren,
aber dieses Jahr muss uns beide weiterbringen."

A few years later he was to discover that there
was nothing so jealous as his work ; that if he was
to satisfy its demands he must make of his life
something as solitary as the life of a monastery.
"Es gibt vielleicht nichts so Eifersüchtiges wie
meinen Beruf ; ... wohl ... muss ich sehen, nach

und nach zu einem Kloster auszuwachsen und so dazustehen in der Welt." This is, in fact, in large measure (although not entirely) the explanation of the almost fanatical demand for solitude which we find insistently reiterated in the letters. Rilke himself called it later his "Einsamkeitsfanatismus." He was not a man who disliked his fellow-men. Rarely have a poet's friends, if we are to believe the records of Rilke's associates, been treated with greater kindness of heart, generosity and delicacy of feeling. Indeed, it was often because he knew that this giving of himself to his friends was so difficult to control that he built walls of solitude about him.

He spent most of the winter of 1906-1907 at Capri with his friend, Frau Faehndrich, who had set aside for his private use the little Rose House in the garden of her villa, which he describes in a delightful letter to his wife. But even there the lack of real solitude irks him. Writing to his Swedish friend, Ellen Key, he says: "Unser kleiner Kreis ist der reizendste, den man sich denken kann, aber für mich ist das so furchtbar schwer, das noch so schöne Beisammen mit Menschen mit wirklicher Arbeit zu vereinen.... Und, unter Menschen, und gerade unter lieben, komm ich so leicht dazu, zu reden und alles

mögliche fortzugeben im Gespräch, was dann wohl
für die Arbeit fehlt. Das ist eine dumme Un-
geschicklichkeit, dass mir so ganz die Gabe der
Geselligkeit fehlt, das Talent zu leichten, gleichsam
erholenden Gesprächen, bei denen man sich nicht
erregt und fortgibt."

What he longed for was to feel himself completely alone; and three days so spent in Naples
he regarded as a priceless treasure: " niemand
als Sie weiss, was ein vollkommenes Alleinsein,
Unbeobachtet-, Ungesehen-, Unsichtbarsein für
mich ist.   Drei Tage in Neapel ging ich damit wie
mit einem Kleinod um in all der herrlich frem-
den Welt. . . ."   We are reminded of Elizabeth
Barrett Browning's lines :

'Tis sublime this perfect solitude of foreign lands.
To be as if you had not been till then
And were then simply what you chose to be.

In attempting to answer one of those unwelcome
enquiries as to ' influences ' which scholars were
beginning to put to him a year or two before his
death, he said that the most important thing of all
was, probably, that he had been alone in so many
places :   " dass ich *allein* sein durfte in so viel
Ländern, Städten und Landschaften, ungestört, mit
der ganzen Vielfalt, mit allem Gehör und Gehorsam

meines Wesens einem Neuen ausgesetzt, willig
ihm zuzugehören und doch wieder genötigt, mich
von ihm abzuheben."

If solitude was indispensable for the absorption
of impressions, it was still more so for the actual
work of creation. He insists in 1906 that what
he needs to enable him to complete his prose work,
Malte Laurids Brigge, is the solitude of Rome,
where it was begun, where he was " allein, nur mit
meiner Frau in der Nachbarschaft, die auch ar-
beitete, so dass wir uns gar nicht täglich sahen,
aber doch einander halfen." The visit to Sweden,
which interrupted this solitude, he describes as
enjoyable, but detrimental to his work : " Ich kam
dann zu Freunden nach Schweden, die mir alles
boten, was die offenste Gastfreundlichkeit geben
kann, aber doch das nicht geben konnten, dieses
unbegrenzte Alleinsein, dieses jeden Tag wie ein
Leben nehmen, dieses Mit-allem-Sein, kurz den
Raum, den man nicht absieht und in dem man
mitten drinnen steht, von Unzähligem umkreist."
That spaciousness in which only the rhythm of
the Eternal Will is felt and human measurement
of time is lost :

> Dein Wille geht wie eine Welle,
> und jeder Tag ertrinkt darin.

It was what he calls " das gründliche Alleinsein "
in the castle of Duino, on the shores of the Adriatic,
which had inspired the first of the great Elegies,
and " das gesteigerte, grosse Alleinsein " of the
Rhone valley which made their completion possible.
It is, he protests, for the sake of his work alone
that he so insists upon solitude : " Meine Arbeit
war immer so sehr vom Alleinsein inspiriert, dass
ich rein positiv, nicht aus Menschenscheu, um
ihretwillen die Stille wünschen muss." Only in
such conditions can he know what he describes
in one of the loveliest lines of the Elegies as :

> Die ununterbrochene Nachricht, die aus Stille sich
> bildet.

The study of Rilke's works will always leave a
sense of the depth and gravity of his outlook on
life as well as of the beauty of his craftmanship.
And learned criticism has rightly confined itself
to the exploration of the origins of this outlook
and the mode of its expression. Perhaps only in
the *Geschichten vom lieben Gott* is there any sign in
his poetic work of that slightly mischievous, at
times ironic, humour which was the delight of his
friends. Just here and there in the letters there
are traces of it, which give us cause to regret that
it never came into its own in his writings. There

is real enjoyment in his thumb-nail sketch of
Bernard Shaw, sitting as a model to Rodin. Shaw's
personality and his whole manner delighted Rilke
greatly, who described him to Clara Rilke as " that
ironical and by no means uncongenial mocker."
Shaw sat to Rodin in the spring of 1906 and came
out daily to the studio at Meudon, bringing his
wife with him. Rilke frequently made one of the
company whilst Rodin was at work. Progress
was rapid. " Das Porträt schreitet ungeheuer vor,
dank der Energie, mit der Shaw steht," writes
Rilke. " Er steht wie ein Ding, das den Willen
hätte zu stehen, noch ausser seiner selbstver-
ständlichen Anlage dazu. Und alles, bis tief aus
seinen langen Beinen her, sammelt sich im Kopf
und im Halse." At the third sitting, to Shaw's
great enjoyment, Rodin made him sit in a small
nursery chair so that he might work at close
quarters on the bust. This was already remarkably
life-like and, when the sculptor took a wire and
proceeded to cut off the head, Shaw watched the
decapitation " mit unbeschreiblicher Freude." One
is tempted to think that, if circumstances had led
Rilke to correspond with " diesem nicht unsym-
pathischen Spötter," we should have had a series
of letters in which a vivid and caustic humour
would have found release. As it is, we must turn

c

for traces of it to such passages as the intimate
description, given to his wife, of their friend, Ellen
Key. This writer, once the leading feminist of
Sweden whose advanced doctrines on educational
reform startled Europe, had become no more than
a mere remnant of an antiquated ideal : " Ach, es
ist eigentlich traurig. Wie sie nichts ist als ein
Fetzchen altmodischen Ideals . . . [eine gute] Aller-
weltstante, die alle Taschen voll hat für die, die an
Zuckerstücken und billigen Bonbons Vergnügen
finden, die aber keinem einzigen den Hunger zu
stillen vermag, mit ihrer armseligen, schon ein
wenig abgelegenen Verköstigung." The week of
their sight-seeing together in Paris was one of very
mixed pleasure for the poet. Particularly their
visit to the Louvre, when the good Ellen had a
ready and stereotyped emotional response—something, he suggests, like a photographic snapshot of
the feelings—for each masterpiece before which
they took their stand. Unfortunately, it was just
one of those days on which Mona Lisa was in a
mood of the most arrogant exclusiveness !

Rilke's sound critical faculty in matters of literature is constantly evident in the letters. Less perhaps during the Paris period, when he immersed
himself in the plastic and graphic arts, than in the
final volumes. He was one of the most acute

critics, if not *the* most acute critic, of his own works. The enormous success of his *Cornet* frankly amused him, for he soon realised that this little work—" dieses höchst nebensächliche Buch " —written in the ardour of youth, was superficial in treatment and lacking in plasticity, as he describes it in a letter to his wife. The *Stunden-Buch*, still perhaps the work most generally thought of in this country when Rilke's name is mentioned, had little interest for him later, because he saw in it only the expression of an out-lived phase of his life. That his own opinion was not at all affected by popular judgment is not surprising, in view of the fact that he defined fame as the sum of the misunderstandings which gather about a new name.

What he says of *Die Aufzeichnungen des Malte Laurids Brigge* is important. It reveals that courageous strain in the writer which, in my opinion, is nowhere more clearly shown than in that sometimes misinterpreted work. The mystical selflessness of the *Stunden-Buch* and the extreme sensitiveness of the *Aufzeichnungen*—they were for many years Rilke's best-known works—did much to establish a totally false conception of his austerely courageous temper. In addition to this, the poet's own belief, constantly reiterated, that he was the last

of an ancient, aristocratic race encouraged interpreters to see in him a rather bloodless decadent,
who dwelt morbidly on the unlovely and was
incapable of answering the challenge of life. Rilke
himself was amongst the first to realise that *Malte*
might easily be thus misunderstood. Many people,
he says, will put this book away as the despairing
work of a writer who has lost courage, and will
fail entirely to recognise that the forces at work
in it are in no sense destructive, despite the fact
that they do, on occasion, lead to destruction :
" das ist die Rückseite jeder grossen Kraft, was das
Alte Testament so ausdrückt, dass es im Grunde
nicht angeht, einen Engel zu sehen, ohne an ihm zu
sterben." And a few days later he writes : " Dass
der arme Malte daran zugrunde geht, ist seine Sache
und braucht uns nicht weiter zu bekümmern.
Wichtig ist nur, dass das Übergrosse nicht ver-
schmäht, sich so vertraut mit uns einzulassen, dies
ist, wie man in einer gewissen Zeit würde gesagt
haben, die Moral des Buchs, die Rechtfertigung
seines Daseins."

There is a notable passage in a letter to his wife,
written in September 1908, in which he describes
himself as sent forth to dwell amongst men in order
to see the whole of life and to avoid or reject
nothing. He sees himself like a man gathering

healing herbs, bent over his task and occupied, to
all appearances, with something of negligible worth,
but the time will come, he says, when he will brew
the draught in which poisonous and deadly elements have their part, and will offer it in its salutary
strength to God so that He may quench His thirst
and feel the glory that flows in His veins. "Ich . . .
bin ausgesandt . . ., um unter dem Menschlichen
zu sein, um alles zu sehen, um nichts abzulehnen,
keine der tausend Verwandlungen, in denen das
Äusserste sich verstellt und schwärzt und unkennt-
lich macht. Ich bin wie einer, der Pilze sammelt
und Heilkräuter unter den Kräutern; da sieht man
gebückt und mit Geringem beschäftigt aus, während die Stämme ringsum stehen und anbeten.
Aber die Zeit wird kommen, wo ich den Trank
bereite. Und die andere, wo ich ihn hinaufbringe,
in dem alles verdichtet ist und verbunden, das
Giftigste und Tödlichste, um seiner Stärke willen;
hinaufbringe zu Gott, damit er seinen Durst stille
und seinen Glanz in seine Adern strömen fühle."
He wrote this after tasting the experiences of Paris
to the full, when he was determined to finish his
Malte Laurids Brigge, begun in Rome in 1904, whatever the handling of the bitter-deadly ingredients
might cost him. "Helft mir," he adds, " so weit
Ihr könnt zu ruhiger Zeit, dass ich meinen Malte

Laurids mache : ich kann nur durch ihn durch weiter, er liegt mir im Weg."

Space does not allow of my dealing here with the illuminating letters in which the Sonnets and the Elegies are discussed. They are, perhaps, the most important letters of the whole collection, as will be shown elsewhere in the present volume, and they reveal the same sense of proportion as is shown in the estimation of his other works. On the completion of the Elegies, he wrote to his most intimate friends with something in the nature of religious thanksgiving that he had won through everything to accomplish this. To the Princess of Thurn and Taxis he wrote on the very day they were finished : " endlich, Fürstin, endlich, der gesegnete, wie gesegnete Tag, da ich Ihnen den Abschluss . . . der Elegien anzeigen kann. . . . Alles in ein paar Tagen, es war ein namenloser Sturm, ein Orkan im Geist . . . alles, was Faser in mir ist und Geweb, hat gekracht,—an Essen war nie zu denken, Gott weiss, wer mich genährt hat. Aber nun *ists*. Ist, Amen. Ich habe also dazu hin überstanden, durch alles hindurch. Durch Alles. Und das wars ja, was not tat. *Nur* dies."

In these letters Rilke has given richly of his spiritual experiences. He has spared no pains in the true and often very beautiful expression of his deepest thought.   He has shown a touching eagerness to understand and adapt himself to the needs of others, especially of those who were younger and perplexed by life, as he himself had often been. In all the letters, even in those addressed to his most familiar friends, there is a touch of old-world courtesy and grace ; and over all there is that delicate veil of reserve which is so characteristic of the man.   Yet he understood and valued friendship as few have done.   Conscious all his life of his homelessness, he found his home, he tells us, in the faith and affection of his friends.   His reserve is but the acknowledgment of that law of restraint which has, from the beginning, been laid upon men.

The embrace of the gods may be strong and possessive.   To man it is given only to lay a light touch on the shoulder of his friend :

Erstaunte euch nicht auf attischen Stelen die Vorsicht
menschlicher Geste ? war nicht Liebe und Abschied
so leicht auf die Schultern gelegt, als wär es aus
    anderm
Stoffe gemacht als bei uns ?   Gedenkt euch der
    Hände,
wie sie drucklos beruhen, obwohl in den Torsen die
    Kraft steht.

Diese Beherrschten wussten damit : so weit sind wirs,
dieses ist unser, uns so zu berühren ; stärker
stemmen die Götter uns an.   Doch *dies* ist Sache der
    Götter.

The portrayal I have attempted is necessarily
inadequate.   It is not easy to accomplish in words
what the visual arts have failed to do.   We know
that the poet himself considered none of his existing portraits to be sufficiently true to life ; none so
valid as that which would remain in the hearts
and memories of his friends.   In his last will and
testament he said : " Von meinen Bildern halte
ich kein anderes für wesentlich gültig, als die bei
einzelnen Freunden, in Gefühl und Gedächtnis,
noch bestehenden."   Those of us who have talked
with friends who knew him best have found that
even they had more to tell than could be said in
words.

RILKE AND THE CONCEPTION
OF DEATH

By WILLIAM ROSE

RILKE AND THE CONCEPTION
OF DEATH

PREOCCUPATION with the thought of death is a remarkable feature of the work of outstanding writers of Rilke's generation, and it is not easy to understand why this should be so without first examining the social and psychological conditions in Germany which were responsible for such a phenomenon. For this purpose it would be necessary to go back at least to the latter part of the eighteenth century, for when one thinks of death as a theme in literature the first names that force themselves on one's mind are those of Schopenhauer, Wagner and Novalis. As such ' Gründlichkeit ' is not possible, however, within the space available for the present study, the matter can only be touched upon briefly.

It has been pointed out recently that the contacts between the German Neo-Romantic writers of the early twentieth century and the Romanticists of a hundred years before were mainly links with Novalis, and that even this relationship is to be

discovered chiefly in their attitude to and artistic
treatment of death.   It is indeed impossible, if we
take four of the most significant writers of our
own age, to discuss the work of Hofmannsthal,
Schnitzler, Thomas Mann or Rilke without becoming immersed in the subject of death as presented in his different way by each of them.   In
Die Welt als Wille und Vorstellung Schopenhauer
asserts that without death there could hardly be
any philosophy—" Der Tod ist der eigentliche
inspirierende Genius der Philosophie. . . . Schwerlich sogar würde auch ohne den Tod philosophiert
werden."   Thomas Mann, who regards death as a
problem of the artist rather than the philosopher,
has given a different turn to this idea, and says
that without death there would be no literature—
" Es würde schwerlich gedichtet werden auf
Erden ohne den Tod."

The attitude to death among German creative
writers varies considerably.   To some extent in
Hofmannsthal, but conspicuously in Thomas Mann,
the influence of the pessimistic philosophy of
Schopenhauer is evident—the view that death
involves annihilation.   Novalis, on the contrary,
regarded death as something desirable, the state in
which he would experience the ultimate fulfilment
of love ; and the poetic idea of the ' Liebestod,'

the union of eroticism and death, which plays such an important part in his work, has found immortal expression in another art form—in the music of Wagner's *Tristan und Isolde*. And though death has no transcendental significance for Thomas Mann, who was influenced more by Schopenhauer than by Novalis, yet in his wonderful story *Tristan* he has interpreted the Liebestod music in words which are themselves like a heavy, sweet narcotic carrying the spirit away in a submerging flood of oblivion.

Of all modern German writers it is Rilke who comes closest to Novalis in the mysticism of his conception, but in the content of that conception he differs materially. For Rilke too death is a goal, but not one to be achieved by mere romantic longing. Death is a condition not to be longed for in a state of the spirit between waking and dreaming, but to be striven for with all the fervour of an inspiring ethical purpose. His conception of death was also bound up indissolubly with an incessant search for contact with God, and his existence in this world of the spirit was encompassed by a loneliness which appears as perhaps the most poignant feature of his poetry.

The attempt to investigate and explain Rilke's conception of death involves therefore the study

of his attitude to God and his conception of
solitude. And it entails more than the study of
a poet's ideas. In the case of Rilke's attitude to
God and death the boundary of thought and feeling is not always sharply outlined. We cannot
draw a definite line between his mental and his
emotional components. The profound and overwhelming experiences of his life—Russia, Rodin
and Paris—were in part intellectual and in part
emotional. The influence of Russia was mainly
emotional, that of Rodin mainly intellectual, and
both have left an indelible stamp on his poetry.
A study of his conception of and attitude to death
is therefore at the same time an approach to an
understanding of his poetic quality. We shall
arrive at a false interpretation of Rilke's poetry if
we merely juggle with such terms as 'mysticism'
or 'religiosity,' without attempting to analyse
his conceptions and to consider him both as a
lonely individual struggling to come to grips with
the meaning of life and as a member of a human
society in which he was ill at ease but which
conditioned the whole of his experience.

In his early volumes of verse we see a phase of
melancholy dreaming and questioning which was
to develop into a tireless wrestling with the two
problems that absorbed his mind and soul. At

this immature stage he wants to be left with his
dreams :

> Was reisst ihr aus meinen blassen, blauen
> Stunden mich in der wirbelnden Kreise
> wirres Geflimmer?
> Ich mag nicht mehr euren Wahnsinn schauen.
> Ich will wie ein Kind im Krankenzimmer
> einsam, mit heimlichem Lächeln, leise,
> leise—Tage und Träume bauen.

In his early letters, diaries and poems he speaks
continually of his solitude.   In one poem it is
' sacred solitude,' in another it is ' pale solitude.'
His longing is ' nächteblass,' he frequently uses
the word ' müde,' a favourite word of many contemporary Austrian poets, and all the elements of
his lonely, weary, dreamy yearning are contained
in the three lines :

> Müd, wie mit scheuem Schwingenschlag,
> durchirren deine Heimwehaugen
> den uferlosen Sonnentag.

Then came his visits to Russia, and these, together with a possible trace of Slav blood in his
veins, of which however we have no evidence,
gave a colouring to his mind and a heightened
emotional receptivity which influenced much of his
work.   He found there solitude and God.   He

spoke of Russia as the land where the people were lonely people, each with a world in himself, each full of darkness like a mountain, each deep in his humbleness, without fear of abasing himself, and therefore pious. People full of remoteness, uncertainty and hope ; people who were still evolving. And over all a never fixed, eternally changing, growing God. Apart from his attraction to the people he was profoundly affected by the landscape, the wide plains and illimitable distances. In both the people and the landscape he found loneliness, the solitude he craved. He said that he wished Russia were his home, that if anything like home could be given to him it would be there, " in diesem weiten leidvollen Land." As late as 1920 he wrote that the Russian has shown that even a state of serfdom and suffering which permanently crushes all powers of resistance does not necessarily effect the destruction of the soul. The Russian soul is able to attain a degree of submission so complete that it acquires a sort of fourth dimension in which, however oppressive circumstances may be, it enters on a new and infinite freedom.

Just as the very enslavement of the soul may be the source of its freedom, so the solitude which Rilke found in Russia, and in which he found

something so profoundly akin to his own nature, is not merely a spiritual vacuum. It is a state of being which may comprise or encompass a complex variety of spiritual experience, and Rilke summed it up in the phrase " Russland grenzt an Gott "— Russia borders on God.

Rilke's search for solitude did not mean that he shut himself off from the world, though one cannot help feeling at times that he was rather intolerant of those of his fellow-men who could not avoid intruding on his privacy when he sought his privacy in public places. When he went on a holiday he did not like to find other holiday-makers there. He had the experienced traveller's contempt of tourists. In one of his letters he complains about the occasional appearance of the inevitable Englishwoman on the beach which prevented him from bathing in the nude. He was, perhaps, more justified in his objection to an American in the writing-room of his hotel who was unable to find a comfortable place to put his feet and looked across from time to time to see whether there was not room for them on Rilke's writing-table. In a letter to Stefan Zweig he wrote, " Jetzt sehe ich niemanden und habe noch für Wochen und Wochen dieses Nichtsehen und Nichtgesehensein innerlich nötig." He never read

D

what critics or elucidators wrote about his work,
and to a correspondent who had published a book
about him he said, " Ich muss mit meiner Arbeit
allein sein und habe so wenig das Bedürfnis, andere
von ihr reden zu hören, wie etwa einer wünschte,
die Urteile anderer über die Frau, die er liebt,
gedruckt zu sehen und zu sammeln." Comments
and criticisms, he said, came between him and his
work ; they were foreign bodies which he would
not assimilate if he could, since that which was
explicit in them would come more and more to
drive out and usurp the unconscious factor in the
intimate and inward relationship by which the
workman and his work are inscrutably bound.
He would not expose this to the jeopardy of published criticism, which he regarded as a letter
addressed to the public and which the author must
not open and read.

Yet his voluminous correspondence with a vast
circle of friends and acquaintances, and the extraordinary number of people who were continually
putting rooms, houses and even mansions at his
disposal for him to live in as long as he liked,
bear witness to his constant contact with the outside world ; though in his published letters, apart
from those written during the War and shortly
afterwards, there is hardly ever a reference to what

was happening in this outside world apart from matters of art.

To Rilke solitude meant the achieving of a state in which his spirit was in complete harmony with itself. Even his marriage he regarded as a means of fortifying his solitude. " Meine mit dem zeitlichen Leben so wenig zusammenhängende Welt war in der Junggesellenstube allen Winden preisgegeben, unumschützt, und bedurfte zu ihrer Entwicklung des stillen eigenen Hauses unter den weiten Himmeln der Einsamkeit." It is true that he ruefully adds that he had read in the writings of a German professor of philosophy how two could live more simply and cheaply than one, and had believed him, but it is characteristic of Rilke that he should have learned of this widespread but mistaken notion through reading the works of a philosopher. When his daughter was born the wall round his solitude seemed completed and rounded off—" da schien der Mauerkreis um die kleine Welt vollendet," and his state of spiritual solitude is again brought into relation with God when he says that it was not the cloistered seclusion of a monastic existence which would be suitable for him, but that he must try himself gradually to grow into a cloister with walls round him and God within him. The same idea is expressed in the words of Emerson which Rilke set as a motto to his book on Rodin—" The hero is he who is immovably centred."

So Rilke ran the whole gamut of the search for solitude, from the sentimental surrender to the pleasurable pain of longing, as in his early poem,

> ich möchte immer weiter schreiten
> bis in das Tal, wo tiefgeschmiegt
> an abendrote Einsamkeiten
> die Sehnsucht wie ein Garten liegt

to a striving for complete isolation in the universe as a means to contact with God.   And he offers up a mystic appeal to God as his only companion in his suffering—" du meines Leidens leiser Zweiter."   God is a part of the poet's solitude —" du bist der zweite seiner Einsamkeit."   It is this which endows his solitude with significance, for it is only to the solitary that revelation is possible—" nur dem Einsamen wird offenbart." Solitude was essential to him, for without it he could not work.   He once said that he had been inwardly dislocated for a time, but his solitude had acted as a kind of spiritual splint in which something had been healed.   It had given him everything, he had wrung from it everything, " was mein ist an Bewusstem und Unbewusstem."

Even in his earlier poems his longing at times acquires an insistency which carries him beyond a state of passive resignation :

> Schau ich die blaue Nacht, vom Mai verschneit,
> in der die Welten weite Wege reisen,
> mir ist : ich trage ein Stück Ewigkeit
> in meiner Brust.   Das rüttelt und das schreit
> und will hinauf und will mit ihnen kreisen . . .
> Und das ist Seele.

He is trying here to give poetic form to profounder longings. The search for God and the later conception of death are already foreshadowed. In a poem entitled *Venedig*, with its vision of himself as a dead emperor being carried to his tomb in a gondola, he dramatises the thought of death, and in *Das Buch der Bilder* he speaks in two poems of death lurking inside us. A girl's death, he says, was already old when her life began, and it attacked that life to prevent it being the survivor :

> dein Tod war schon alt,
> als dein Leben begann ;
> drum griff er es an,
> damit es ihn nicht überlebte.

And turning the old aphorism which warns us that ' in the midst of life we are in death,' he declares that in the midst of life death is in us :

> Der Tod ist gross.
> Wir sind die Seinen
> lachenden Munds.
> Wenn wir uns mitten im Leben meinen,
> wagt er zu weinen
> mitten in uns.

Already in these earlier poems he pictures death as something which is fully developed within us and awaiting its moment to emerge. Later his conception underwent a change and he regarded death as being capable of growth, and it is in the third part of his cycle of poems *Das Stunden-Buch*, together with his prose work *Die Aufzeichnungen des Malte Laurids Brigge*, that we find his attitude to death so copiously illustrated that it is possible to state his conception as a formula. He postulates two kinds of death, which he calls " der grosse Tod " and " der kleine Tod," or " der eigne Tod " and " der fremde Tod." The meaning of these terms will be seen in a moment.

In the third part of the *Stunden-Buch*, which is devoted to the mysteries of death and poverty, the poet speaks of the fear which comes over him in large towns. In a number of poems he pictures the misery of those who live in cities, the children who do not know that flowers outside are calling to freedom and happiness, the virgins whose long-

ings are unfulfilled and who come to motherhood
in a wretched environment, the people whose days
are lived degradingly in the service of things that
have no meaning and who wait in suspense and
dread for the day when they will be admitted to
a hospital where death will come to them. They
are oppressed by a world which brings them to
their death without their ever having understood
the meaning of life :

> Da leben Menschen, weisserblühte, blasse,
> und sterben staunend an der schweren Welt.

The death they die is " der kleine Tod," part of an
anonymous mass production of death of which
Rilke gives an example in *Malte*.   In the ancient
Hôtel-Dieu in Paris, he says, people used to die in
a few beds.   " Jetzt wird in 559 Betten gestorben.
Natürlich fabrikmässig.   Bei so enormer Pro-
duktion ist der einzelne Tod nicht so gut ausge-
führt, aber darauf kommt es auch nicht an.   Die
Masse macht es.   Wer gibt heute noch etwas für
einen gut ausgearbeiteten Tod? Niemand.   Sogar
die Reichen, die es sich doch leisten könnten,
ausführlich zu sterben, fangen an nachlässig und
gleichgültig zu werden ; der Wunsch, einen eigenen
Tod zu haben, wird immer seltener."
   It is Rilke's idea that each individual contains

within himself his own death, peculiar to himself, which grows and matures as he grows and matures. It may, however, never come to maturity, as in the case of the poor people of his poems. And he pleads to God to give everyone his own death:

> O Herr, gib jedem seinen eignen Tod,
> das Sterben, das aus jenem Leben geht,
> darin er Liebe hatte, Sinn und Not.
>
> Denn wir sind nur die Schale und das Blatt.
> Der grosse Tod, den jeder in sich hat,
> das ist die Frucht, um die sich alles dreht.

" Der eigne Tod " is the personal death which is the eventual fulfilment of a personal life, but which few men experience. Most people suffer merely " den kleinen Tod," an alien death. Lives which have known no fulfilment come to a close in a death which likewise is not a fulfilment.

A personal death does not come to an individual in the natural course of things. He must so mould his life that his death will come in a personal and not a mass, or impersonal, form. Rilke realised that each man's life is essentially only his own. Similarly with his death. A man's death is also essentially his own. All the experiences of a man's soul are linked with one another, and the final experience is death, which is linked with all the others. It exerts a retroactive influence on his life, and is therefore of the utmost significance for that life. It follows that if a man possesses the power to shape his living experience, he also has the power to shape his ultimate experience, which is death. Hence Rilke's abhorrence of mass living, which involves an eventual mass death. He believed that a man *can* shape and perfect his spiritual experience, and therefore that he is able to shape and perfect his death too. He must consequently see to it that he takes an active share in determining the form of this ultimate experience, that he does not die merely the death which is the usual conclusion of a particular disease, being something which is outside his own inner nature and having no relation to his own inner self. The death he dies must be familiar to him and not something alien; it must be essentially personal.

In an early entry in his diary Rilke says, " Wer den Tod nur recht versteht und feiert, der macht auch das Leben gross." Though the thought and feeling of death should have such a great part in a man's spiritual life, since this is a constant preparation for an " eigener Tod," death has an ethical or educative significance for life itself, since preoccupation with it affects the nature of the values

one sees in life. Its effect on life is not merely
negative or destructive, but it is a positive experience for which life is a preparation, and it therefore
exercises a fruitful influence on the life of which
it is the climax. Our effort to mature a personal
death implies that we are at the same time maturing
a personal life.

There is a book by the German philosopher,
Georg Simmel, which throws a certain light on
Rilke's conception of a personal death. In his
book on Rembrandt, which he calls an essay in
the philosophy of art, Simmel refers to the Greek
conception of the Parcæ, who abruptly cut the
thread of life. This, he says, involves the idea
that life is exclusively life, having in it no element
of death, but destined at a certain point along its
path, and at that point only, to come into contact
with it. This is very different from the idea that
death is inherent in life from the outset, which
Simmel holds to be the truer conception, since
there can be no doubt that death is an ever-present
inner reality without which our lives would be
unimaginably different from what they are. Death
is a quality of organic existence, and Simmel asserts
that this conception of death can be seen in the
most profound portraits of Rembrandt. They
contain life in its widest sense, which includes

the immanence of death. In the case of many Italian portraits one has the impression that the subjects of them are likely to meet their end at the point of a stiletto. In the case of Rembrandt's portraits one feels that the person's eventual death will be a consequential development of the totality of his life ; as a river, merging at last into the sea, is not overwhelmed by a foreign element, but pursues to the end the natural flow which was inherent in it from its source.

As in Rembrandt's portraits, so in Shakespeare's tragedies. In the case of Shakespeare's tragic heroes death is, as it were, an *a priori* determining factor of their lives ; the maturing of their destiny is at the same time a maturing of their death. The poisoned rapier which kills Hamlet is so fortuitous an expedient, that it is obviously not the manner of his death which matters, but only its symbolic significance.

Shakespeare's tragic heroes, says Simmel, are great individuals, as distinguished from his comic characters, who are types, and he points to the relationship which exists between individuality and death. Only the individual dies, not the type. Classical art sought to bridge the antithesis between the mortality of the subject and the immortality of its expression in art by lifting the subject into the sphere of timelessness, and the way in which this was achieved was by presenting it as a type. German art, on the other hand, is individualistic; it strives towards infinity and is perhaps nourished, suggests Simmel, by the irreconcilability between individuality, in which death is an inherent factor, and art which, purely as art, stands above death. And he points to the lines of Rilke which have already been quoted above as the supreme refinement in lyric poetry of the conception of individuality :

> O Herr, gib jedem seinen eignen Tod,
> das Sterben, das aus jenem Leben geht,
> darin er Liebe hatte, Sinn und Not.

In these lines Simmel sees confirmed his view that death loses its commonplace and uniform quality when it ceases to be, like the medieval symbol of the skeleton, merely a contrast to life. In the measure in which it becomes personal to the individual, in the measure in which each one dies ' his own death,' it becomes an essential element in life itself.

If Simmel is right, then Rilke stands in the line of a great tradition, though this in no way detracts from his poetic originality. His conception of death as a stage in our development is closely

linked with a further idea which inspired some of
the most striking poetry of the *Stunden-Buch*. He
regarded the evolution of man as a factor in the
evolution of God. He said that the faults, the
injustice, together with the insufficiency of power
of God lie in His evolution, since He is not yet
perfected. Man needed God so urgently that he
was sensible of Him from the very beginning as
a Being in existence. Man needed Him complete
and said, " God is." Now God has to catch up
with this premature completion of His development, and it is we who help Him to do so. He
evolves as we evolve, He grows with our joys
and the shadows on His countenance are caused
by our griefs. After we have found ourselves,
everything we do affects Him. And the poet
draws strength from the consciousness that the
individual, with his qualities and reactions, is important for God. A poetic counterpart of this
entry in his diary is to be seen in the lines of
the *Stunden-Buch*—

> mit meinem Reifen
> reift
> dein Reich.

In the poems of the *Stunden-Buch* Rilke every-
where insists that God depends on man as much

as man depends on God, that the one has no
meaning without the other—

> denn wer bin ich und wer bist du,
> wenn wir uns nicht verstehn ?

He even asks what God will do when he, the poet,
is dead.

> Was wirst du tun, Gott, wenn ich sterbe ?
> Ich bin dein Krug (wenn ich zerscherbe ?)
> Ich bin dein Trank (wenn ich verderbe ?)
> Bin dein Gewand und dein Gewerbe,
> mit mir verlierst du deinen Sinn.

And he concludes :

> Was wirst du tun, Gott ?   Ich bin bange.

This is not altogether a new thought in German
literature, though it had never been transmuted
into such magnificent poetry.   Angelus Silesius,
the Catholic mystic of the seventeenth century,
expressed a similar idea in ever-varying form in the
couplets of *Der Cherubinische Wandersmann* :

> Ich weiss, dass ohne mich Gott nicht ein Nu kann
>   leben ;
> werd' ich zunicht', Er muss vor Not den Geist auf-
>   geben.

It must be noted that whereas Angelus Silesius
declares that God ceases to exist when His relation

to the individual disappears, Rilke asserts only
that God loses His meaning.   But there is not,
perhaps, very much difference between the two
attitudes, for these poems of Rilke are as much the
precipitate of a torturing search for God as an
expression of faith in His existence.   In so far as
Rilke realises the presence which he calls God in
the phenomena of Nature and in things he is a
pantheist, but his awareness of this presence, his
contact with it, is achieved by intensity of feeling
and not by intellectual perception.   And he identi-
fies God and life rather than God and Nature.
He said in one of his letters that love of life and
love of God must coincide : that by living life to
perfection we are worshipping and creating God.
Here we see the relation to his conception of
death as an experience which we can help to form
by the way we live our lives.   We can not only
help to develop and perfect our death, we can also
help to develop and perfect God, and this latter idea
is the inspiration of poems in the *Stunden-Buch* in
which he compares God to a cathedral and humanity
to the builders :

> Wir bauen an dir mit zitternden Händen,
> und wir türmen Atom auf Atom.
> Aber wer kann dich vollenden,
> du Dom.

In Rilke's theory of death and his view of the evolution of man as an essential factor in the evolution of God, there is something analogous to the Buddhist philosophy of death as a recurring stage in man's cycle before his eventual absorption in the universal soul, but it must be admitted that the analogy cannot be pressed very far.

We have seen the relationship between God, death and solitude in Rilke's outlook. In the third part of the *Stunden-Buch* death is further linked with poverty. Poverty is not only a state of not having, just as death is not only a state of not being. It is " ein grosser Glanz aus Innen." Poverty and solitude are significant if we consider them not as forms of deprivation, but as states of being in which the spirit can find the only fitting condition for its development, and death is significant if we regard it not as a ceasing to be, but as the state of being towards the achievement of which one's whole life must be directed.

In Rilke's writings, including his letters, we find the constant iteration of physical and spiritual weariness, and a number of critics have spoken of his 'Todessehnsucht.' This cannot be justified. It is arguable that his craving and lifelong striving for contact with God were of such a nature that

they could only be fulfilled, if at all, in death, but
they were a craving and striving for the reality at
the heart of shifting phenomena.   If death is to be
regarded as the final blossoming of life, something
to which we are working up and not a running
down of the machine, it must logically be something more than mere annihilation.   Though Rilke
condemns modern civilisation he does not repudi-
ate life itself, and he is absorbed in the problem
of death because he regards it as a fulfilment of
life.   He often compares the process of death to
the process of birth.   Dying is only difficult and
foreign to us when it is not " der grosse Tod,"
when it is " der kleine Tod " which comes and
takes us because our own has not matured :

> Denn dieses macht das Sterben fremd und schwer,
> dass es nicht *unser* Tod ist ; einer, der
> uns endlich nimmt, nur weil wir keinen reifen.

Once, when he was in serious financial need, he
referred in one of his letters to his father's desire
to obtain for him a post in a bank in Prague.   That
would mean, he said, spiritual renunciation, " ein
Frost, in dem alles sterben müsste."   He could not
pursue his art, as his father thought ought to be
possible, during his evening leisure.   He would
have to abandon the path that he had followed

E

since his boyhood, the obeying of his impulses and longings; he would have to leave the stones, already hewn and prepared by his own hand for the building up of his life, lying on the ground in order to carry factory-made bricks for the construction of a strange house which meant nothing to him. It would mean jumping out of his boat, which a few strong pulls at the oar might bring to a land of his own, and continuing his journey lost amid the hundreds of passengers on a great liner, to arrive eventually at some common destination as neutral and banal as a tea-garden on a Sunday afternoon. And he concludes, "Ich möchte eher verhungern mit den Meinen, als diesen Schritt tun, der wie ein Tod ist ohne die Grösse des Todes." There is therefore not only the antithesis of a personal and a petty death. There is also the antithesis of a personal and a petty life, and it is because Rilke wished to achieve a personal life that he tried to understand the nature and significance of death. It is true that in his early poems there was an immature yearning for death as an expression of the unwillingness to face life:

> Ich wollt, sie hätten statt der Wiege
> mir einen kleinen Sarg gemacht,
> dann wär mir besser wohl, dann schwiege
> die Lippe längst in feuchter Nacht.

> Dann hätte nie ein wilder Wille
> die bange Brust durchzittert,—dann
> wärs in dem kleinen Körper stille,
> so still, wie's niemand denken kann.

But this was a passing phase. He always shrank from the violence and roughness of life, but later on there is no longing for death in his writings unless, perhaps, as a subconscious element in the haunting fear which pervades *Malte*. Even in the early period his stories show that he recognised the abundance that life has to offer if only one is capable of grasping it. In *Heiliger Frühling*, which tells how the character of a young student is changed through his friendship with an invalid girl, the student tells his companions after the girl's death, " Glaubt mir, es kommt darauf an, dass man einmal im Leben einen heiligen Frühling hat, der einem so viel Licht und Glanz in die Brust senkt, dass er ausreicht, alle ferneren Tage damit zu vergolden." In the sketch *Im Leben* a young official complains of the sedentary life that he and his colleagues are compelled to lead. " Man sollte von uns nicht sagen : sitzende Lebensweise ; denn das ist ein Selbstmord und heisst höchstens : sitzende Todesart." And he says that one does not immediately find one's way to the fulfilment of life, but though it is full of hazards it has so much to offer that one has not enough hands to hold it all or enough eyes to admire—" man tappt so eine Weile herum an der Tür, man findet nicht gleich ins Leben hinein. Und dann ist es ja auch die Gefahr, dieses Leben. Es ist eben Gipfel und Abgrund, Insel und Welle—alles. Alles ! Fühlen Sie, was das heisst ? Das will sagen : Christabend, Bescherung.—Oh, man hat ja gar nicht genug Hände, um alle Gaben zu halten, nicht genug Augen, sie zu bewundern—überhaupt, man ist arm vor Reichtum."

This does not look as though Rilke's interest in death was a denial of the value of life. On the contrary, he believed that it is our very aware-ness of death which intensifies our awareness of life. He spoke of " das erste grosse Ergriffensein vom Bewusstsein des Todes, welches zugleich der erste Moment gesteigerten, allseitigen persönlichen Lebens ist." And the same idea, that an existence without ultimate death is an existence without life, appears in the tenth of the *Duineser Elegien*. From the ethical point of view, we see him in his letters coming to an ever clearer realisation of the signi-ficance of death for one's attitude to the obligations of life. " Ich habe in den letzten Jahren so viel nahe Todeserfahrungen erlernen müssen, aber es ist mir keiner genommen worden, ohne dass ich nicht

die Aufgaben um mich herum vermehrt gefunden
hätte. Die Schwere dieses Unaufgeklärten und vielleicht Allergrössten, das nur durch ein Missver-
ständnis in den Ruf gekommen ist, willkürlich und
grausam zu sein, drückt uns (so mein ich immer
mehr) gleichmässiger und tiefer ins Leben hinein
und legt uns die äussersten Verpflichtungen auf
die langsam wachsenden Kräfte."

Rilke's preoccupation with death is therefore by
no means to be interpreted as an escape from life.
The reverse is the truth. It was only by coming
to grips with the problem of death that life was for
him worth living. The two are not rivals, but
complementary. Again we can quote evidence
from his early writings : " Es bestehen geheime
Beziehungen zwischen dem Schönen und dem
Schrecklichen, an einer bestimmten Stelle ergänzen
sich beide wie das lachende Leben und der nahe
tägliche Tod." " Niemand [kann] auf Ehre und
Gewissen sagen, ob der Tod des Lebens Wider-
sacher ist." " Ich glaube, dass das Leben stärker
ist als der Tod." And in one of his last poetic
cycles, *Die Sonette an Orpheus*, he uses Orpheus, who
went with his lyre to the underworld to fetch back
Euridice, as a symbol of the interrelation of life
and death. He proclaims that only he who has
eaten of the poppy with the dead, only he who is

aware of the dual realm of the dead and the living,
may with full understanding sing in praise of life :

> Nur wer die Leier schon hob
> auch unter Schatten,
> darf das unendliche Lob
> ahnend erstatten.
>
> Nur wer mit Toten vom Mohn
> ass, von dem ihren,
> wird nicht den leisesten Ton
> wieder verlieren.
>
> Mag auch die Spieglung im Teich
> oft uns verschwimmen :
> Wisse das Bild.
>
> Erst in dem Doppelbereich
> werden die Stimmen
> ewig und mild.

In approaching the study of a poet from whose
mind the question of death was never absent, it is
natural to seek for morbid elements both in his
ideas and in his poetry. It may be said at once
that Rilke's conception of death as deduced from
his poetry is not morbid, but when we look at his
most important work in prose, *Die Aufzeichnungen
des Malte Laurids Brigge*, we see that it is pervaded
by apprehension and abounds in descriptions of

the macabre. Shortly after his last sojourn in Paris and a year before his death, Rilke wrote to his friend and translator Maurice Betz to explain why he had left suddenly without having come to say good-bye: "Le sort a quelquefois de ces trous où l'on disparaît; le mien s'appelle malaise, maladie... que sais-je." This *malaise* is seen in its most extreme form in *Malte*.

Malte is the study of a mind in the thrall of an 'anxiety neurosis,' and to understand its relation to Rilke's personal experience, for it contains much of an autobiographical nature, we must go back to his first visit to Paris in 1902. When Rilke first thought of going to Paris he wrote that he would find solitude there. He was feeling deeply the failure of a play which he had had produced in Berlin. He was conscious of his mission as a poet, but felt that he was not understood by the public, and our inkling of his state of mind at this time is substantiated by the evidence he has given us of the effect upon him of his first experience of Paris. This evidence we find both in *Malte* and in his letters, some of which, in fact, he used as material for the book.

His first impression was coloured by the numerous hospitals. "Mich ängstigen," he wrote to his wife, " die vielen Hospitäler, die hier überall sind·

Ich verstehe, warum sie bei Verlaine, bei Baude-
laire und Mallarmé immerfort vorkommen. Man
sieht Kranke, die hingehen oder hinfahren, in
allen Strassen.... Man fühlt auf einmal, dass es
in dieser weiten Stadt Heere von Kranken gibt,
Armeen von Sterbenden, Völker von Toten." He
had never felt that in any other town, and he
says it was strange that he felt it just in Paris
where the life urge was stronger than elsewhere.
It was not life, for life is something calm, spacious,
simple. The life urge is hurry and pursuit, the urge
to possess life at once, wholly, concentrated in an
hour. Of this Paris was full and that was why it
was in such close proximity to death. Again he
says that Paris seemed to him to be rushing along
like a star that had lost its way, heading for some
fearful collision. In the *Stunden-Buch* he speaks of
" die tiefe Angst der übergrossen Städte," and to
his friend Lou Andreas-Salomé he wrote that Paris
was a similar experience to the military academy
of his boyhood, the devastating effect of which he
has described for us elsewhere ; the frightened
wonder of the boy was paralleled by the horror of
the man at the unutterable confusion of life. The
military school and the city had both brought him
into touch with a brusque reality, and in each case
he shrank from the contact. He was alone among

the crowds, the vehicles in the streets passed right through him, and those which were in a hurry did not make a detour round him but ran over him contemptuously. Often, before falling asleep, he would read the thirtieth chapter of the Book of Job, and everything in it was true of himself, word for word. Much of this long and deeply interesting letter appears again in *Malte*, and it is significant that the address at the head of the book, the rue Toullier, is the same as that at which Rilke himself lodged when he first arrived in Paris.

Malte is from the north, a Dane, the last surviving member of an ancient noble family, living alone in a room in Paris. The book is an amalgam of observation and introspection, the association of ideas leading Rilke constantly to hover between the depiction of actual experience and the revelation of inmost thoughts and feelings. It consists mainly of descriptions of Malte's reactions to Paris and reminiscences of his boyhood, his mind being haunted by ghosts of the past, and in the accounts of his early life in an old ancestral mansion ghosts actually appear and are taken as a matter of course. There is even the ghost of a house which had been burnt down, but which both the boy and his mother are convinced can still be seen. This absorption of Malte in his childhood, with all the uncanny details that surge up in his memory, has a bearing on a matter which may be of profound significance for an understanding of Rilke's psychology. It has already been mentioned that in some of Rilke's poetry a connection appears between the two terminal experiences of birth and death. We are told that Rilke was born prematurely. He came into the world two months too soon, and it is possible that this congenital defect influenced his future mentality, that he never overcame psychologically the original shock of birth. His shrinking from the roughness of life, his withdrawal into a world of his own, the nostalgia which found its expression in a restless search for contact with God and an understanding of the problem of death, are susceptible of a psycho-analytical interpretation which is beyond the scope of this essay. Some light is thrown on this aspect of his psychology by the passage in *Malte* which relates how the child would pretend to be a girl, to whom he gave the name Sophie, and would tell his mother about the misdeeds of a certain naughty boy named Malte. And Rilke's biographer, his son-in-law, tells us that the poet himself was brought up like a girl until his fifth year, being dressed in girl's clothes, wearing long hair, and playing with dolls, and that he was kept aloof from children of his

own age. He even once came into his mother's
room pretending to be a girl, and announced his
intention of staying with her since René (this was
his original name : he changed it to Rainer later on)
was a good-for-nothing and had been sent away.
If there is anything in the suggestion that Rilke
was from the first incompletely adapted to life,
there can be little doubt that his early upbringing
fostered a disinclination to face the world.

The most striking example of the atmosphere
which pervades the book is the passage in which
Malte describes how, as he lay in bed, old fears of
his childhood returned—the fear that a thread of
wool frayed from the edge of his blanket might
be hard and sharp like a steel needle ; that a button
on his nightshirt was larger than his head and
heavy ; that a breadcrumb falling from his bed
would turn to glass and smash when it reached
the floor, and that with it everything would be
smashed for ever ; that the edge of an opened
letter was tabu, something that nobody must see,
something indescribably valuable, for which nowhere in the room was safe ; that he might swallow
a piece of coal in his sleep ; that a number in his
mind would grow till there was no more room for
it inside him ; that he was lying on grey granite ;
that he might scream and bring a crowd of people

who would break open the door; that he might betray himself and say things he was afraid of; that he might not be able to say anything since everything is unutterable. He concludes by saying that he had prayed for his childhood and it had returned, but he felt that it was still as oppressive as it had been in reality and that he had not benefited by growing older.

Malte's realisation that he "had not benefited by growing older" summarises in one pregnant sentence the theme of the book—the maladjustment to life of an artist, the last descendant of a decaying race. We think of Thomas Mann's *Buddenbrooks* and of the interest which the novelist shares with the poet not only in the phenomenon of decay, but in death and the manner of dying. A certain taste for the macabre, which is noticeable occasionally in Rilke's poems, reappears in *Malte*, both in the description of horrors and in the accounts of the way people die. We have seen what he thought of the commonplace or impersonal deaths in the Paris hospitals. In the long-drawn-out end of Malte's grandfather, the masterful old Kammerherr Brigge, which was difficult and awe-inspiring, Rilke describes a 'personal' death almost as though it were a banshee that dominated the house and the whole countryside during the

days and nights that the old man lay dying. "Das
war nicht der Tod irgendeines Wassersüchtigen,
das war der böse, fürstliche Tod, den der Kammerherr sein ganzes Leben lang in sich getragen und
aus sich genährt hatte. Alles Übermass an Stolz,
Willen und Herrenkraft, das er selbst in seinen
ruhigen Tagen nicht hatte verbrauchen können,
war in seinen Tod eingegangen. . . . Wie hätte
der Kammerherr Brigge den angesehen, der von
ihm verlangt hätte, er solle einen anderen Tod
sterben, als diesen. Er starb seinen schweren Tod."
Malte talks too of the death of his grandmother,
his father and mother, and many others ; of his
fear at the sudden death of a girl who sat opposite
him in a tram at Naples, of his fear at the death of
his dog, of his fear when the flies came into his
room in autumn after the first night-frosts and
slowly died all over the room, of the nights when
he would sit up oppressed by fear and cling to the
thought that sitting was at least something one did
when one was alive—that dead men do not sit.

We see Rilke a prey to a deep-seated fear of
both visible and invisible terrors. The book is to
a great extent a looking back on childhood, and he
was able to write it by a process of intense introspection which put the rational and the irrational
on the same plane. The characters that appear in

it, those of the past and those of the present, are as real to Malte as his own actual experiences and impressions. As Rilke said in a letter to his Polish translator, they are symbols of Malte's own distress, and his relation to them is conditioned by the fact that the intensity of their lives displays the same rate of vibration as his own. Life is always withdrawing into a state of invisibility, and Malte can only achieve contact with it by conjuring up phenomena and scenes which he finds either in memories of his childhood, in his Parisian environment, or in reminiscences of his reading. All these varieties of experience possess the same validity for him, they are all equally present and permanent. Past fears, present terrors and presentiments of the future are all equally real.

However much Rilke may later have achieved a more balanced relation to life, *Malte* is the creation of a mind that was at the time full of morbid fears. Even in his letters at this period we find him complaining, for example, with reference to a train journey between the French frontier and Turin that the high mountains made the way seem like a tunnel. Of a return journey by the same route he says, " die Tunnels . . . waren lang und quälend." He had never been to London, but the very thought of it was appalling—" Unter

London stelle ich mir etwas sehr Quälendes vor. Sie kennen meine Furcht vor den sehr grossen Städten." We may, perhaps, bring the accusations which he launches against the crowded cities into line with this tormenting fear of tunnels. Both in the *Stunden-Buch* and in *Malte* he declares that it is the cities which make it impossible for men's lives to come to fruition, and that by the inhibiting of their lives their deaths too are inhibited.

Rilke once thought of undergoing psycho-analytical treatment, so he must have realised the neurotic element in his make-up. Two years after the publication of *Malte* he wrote to Lou Andreas-Salomé: " Du begreifst, dass der Gedanke, eine Analyse durchzumachen, mir ab und zu aufsteigt ; zwar ist mir, was ich von Freuds Schriften kenne, unsympathisch und stellenweise haarsträubend ; aber die Sache selbst, die mit ihm durchgeht, hat ihre echten und starken Seiten." Profoundly uneasy as he was, however, about his physical and nervous condition, he fought shy of the prospect of being left with what he called a ' disinfected soul.' He said that psycho-analysis could only help him if he were to make up his mind to give up writing. Then he could have the devils driven out of him, since devils are only a disturbing

factor in a bourgeois existence, and if his angels
happened to be driven out as well, then that too
would have to be regarded as a simplification and
he would console himself with the thought that
in his next profession, if any, he would have no
use for them anyway. He very soon decided,
however, not to submit to treatment. He said
that he was not going to risk the possibility of his
angels being given a fright.

To say that Rilke gave full vent in this book
to the fears which haunted him is not completely
to identify him with Malte Laurids Brigge. We
are, however, justified in suggesting that in the
creation of a fictitional character he was able to
allow freer rein to his apprehensions and obses-
sions than was possible in his lyrical utterances or
his letters. Rilke is not Malte, but there is more
than sufficient evidence of the important autobiographical element. It is not only of Malte's
distress that the characters in the book are symbols.
The whole uneasy atmosphere of the book bears
witness to Rilke's own brooding mind, and no
German author has given us in fiction form a more
ruthless self-revelation since that most remarkable
book of the eighteenth century, *Anton Reiser*.

Malte was his last major work for over a decade,

which included the War years. To his friend and
hostess at Duino he wrote, " Mir graut ein bisschen,
wenn ich an all die Gewaltsamkeit denke, die ich
im Malte Laurids durchgesetzt habe, wie ich mit
ihm in der konsequenten Verzweiflung bis hinter
alles geraten war, bis hinter den Tod gewissermassen, sodass nichts mehr möglich war, nicht
einmal das Sterben." In the *Duineser Elegien* he
at last reached a stage of reconciliation to life
which he was enabled to express with an unsur-
passed mastery of poetic language and symbolism.
It is, perhaps, too much to claim, as some com-
mentators have done, that he had at last rid himself
of the haunting fear and burden of death. The
theme still occupied him, but the *Sonette an Orpheus*
and the *Duineser Elegien* are his final poetic utterance of the outlook on life and death to which
he had won through, with his conception of the
wider sphere, the ' dual realm,' which embraced
them both. Both in form and content they
reveal the achievement of a tranquillity of spirit
such as is seen nowhere else in his poetry or his
prose, and he declared himself that his work was
finished with the creation of the Elegies, that what
he had to say he had now said. Both the Sonnets
and the Elegies sprang from the same creative im-
pulse which moved him after years of comparative

F

poetic sterility, and their significance as his spiritual testament cannot be better expressed than in the words of an explanatory letter he wrote a year before his death. In the Elegies, he said, the affirmation of life and the affirmation of death are one; death is the aspect of life which is turned away from and unillumined by us; there is neither a here nor a beyond, but only the great unity— " In den Elegien wird ... das Leben wieder möglich, ja es erfährt hier diejenige endgültige *Bejahung,* zu der es der junge Malte ... noch nicht führen konnte. *Lebens- und Todesbejahung erweist sich als Eines in den Elegien.* Das eine zuzugeben ohne das andere, sei, so wird hier erfahren und gefeiert, eine schliesslich alles Unendliche ausschliessende Einschränkung. Der Tod ist die uns abgekehrte, von uns unbeschienene *Seite des Lebens* : wir müssen versuchen, das grösseste Bewusstsein unseres Daseins zu leisten, das in *beiden unabgegrenzten Bereichen* zu Hause ist, *aus beiden unerschöpflich genährt.* . . . Die wahre Lebensgestalt reicht durch *beide* Gebiete, das Blut des grössesten Kreislaufs treibt durch *beide* : *es gibt weder ein Diesseits noch Jenseits, sondern die grosse Einheit."* This unity of the state of life and the state of death implies some form of survival, and even of individual survival, but Rilke gives us no indication of his

views on the form which that survival is likely
to take.

I have tried to present a picture, limited necessarily by the nature of my theme, of a poet who
was wholly concentrated on the quest for contact
with the presence, or force, that lies at the springs
of life—a quest which involved him in an anguish
of mind for which he found relief only in his
inspiration and absorption in his poetry.   He
excluded, so far as he could, the bustling life of
his age, to which he never became adjusted—to
which he made no attempt to adjust himself.   The
more closely men are herded together, the more
lonely they can become.   He said himself, " ich
bin ein Ungeschickter des Lebens."   Yet though
there is much that is timeless in the spirit of Rilke,
there is also much that is rooted in the age in which
he lived.   To understand his mind aright we must
consider his environment as well as his personality, the social atmosphere as well as the psychological pattern.   The impact of a mass-producing
civilisation on Rilke's sensitive nature left its
indelible stamp on his spiritual activity and therefore on his poetry.   He did not retire to lonely
places merely in order to dream.   He sought con-
verse with eternity, striving to achieve within

himself the creative solitude by which alone he could attain contact with the presence that he called God and an anticipatory comprehension of the experience of death.   The path which he pursued towards his goal is marked with some of the most original and imperishable poetry that has ever been written in the German tongue.

THE *NEUE GEDICHTE*

By C. M. BOWRA

THE *NEUE GEDICHTE*

UNLIKE his contemporary Stefan George, Rilke seems never to have found a potent inspiration in the life and literature of Germany. The two countries which made the strongest appeal to him and had the greatest influence on his art were Russia and France. It was his visit to Russia which inspired *Das Stunden-Buch* ; it was the years he spent with Rodin in Paris which helped him to write his *Neue Gedichte*. The difference between these works shows how much his circumstances affected Rilke and how intensely he appreciated two widely different civilisations. What he admired in Russia was the old Holy Russia, the country of saints and pilgrims, of simple faith and longing for some degree of absorption in the divine being. In the *Stunden-Buch* he dramatised himself in a rôle that enabled him to express half-hidden thoughts and desires which might seem alien and inappropriate to a cultivated citizen of Central Europe, but were entirely right for a lonely, contemplative Russian monk. The *Stunden-Buch* marked for him the end of an epoch. When he had written it, he

seems to have felt that for the time being he had
written enough in lyric form about himself and his
own feelings. He was indeed to return years
afterwards to the poetry of the self and to revive
in a new form some of the ideas which may be
seen in the *Stunden-Buch*, but in the interval he
turned to a different kind of poetry, to something
more objective, less personal, and in some senses
less intimate.

The causes and character of the change are somewhat complex. Rilke seems to have felt that he had
said all that could be said about his feelings, that
to continue writing as he had hitherto written must
mean the repetition of what he had already done,
and from this his artistic conscience revolted. He
needed a new outlet for his energies, and he found
it in France. The precise direction which his art
now took was to some extent determined by his
admiration for Rodin. He was deeply interested
in sculpture, and in Rodin he saw a great creative
genius who towered above contemporary artists by
the strength and independence of his work. For
some months he lived in Rodin's house, and the
close contact which he found there with another
art than his own affected him in a remarkable way.
He saw that Rodin's sculpture was largely the result
of a great tradition, and to the masterpieces of this

tradition, whether Greek or Medieval, he brought the full powers of his studious, perceptive and devoted mind. Instead of living among dreams he lived among works of visual art until, by a natural process, he wished to make his own poems like them—self-sufficient, perfectly wrought and rich in content. He had indeed attempted something of the same kind in *Das Buch der Bilder*, where in a number of descriptive poems he achieved a degree of objectivity which seems a foreshadowing of what was to come. But the peculiar character of the *Neue Gedichte* does not lie simply in their being more objective than Rilke's earlier poetry. These poems were written with a different conception of the nature of poetry, and in consequence they are fuller and finer than anything he had yet written. They move to a different rhythm ; they are more concentrated, more vivid, more visual. And, what is more remarkable, they were largely written in accordance with a theory of poetry.

Poets are seldom successful when they shape their work to suit a theory of what poetry is or ought to be. Either, like Wordsworth, they write their best by defying their professed aims or, like Mallarmé, they treat their theory so seriously that it becomes too strong for them and stifles their fresh impulses. But when Rilke wrote his *Neue*

Gedichte, he abandoned his earlier instinctive method of composition and wrote with a conscious and definite aim. Two statements of his show what he thought. In *Die Aufzeichnungen des Malte Laurids Brigge* he discusses the nature of poetry and says : " Verses are not, as some people imagine, simply feelings (these we have soon enough) : they are experiences." And in *Requiem* he says :

> O alter Fluch der Dichter,
> die sich beklagen, wo sie sagen sollten,
> die immer urteiln über ihr Gefühl,
> statt es zu bilden.

From these two texts Rilke's theory may be gathered. He was, in the first place, abandoning a view which he had held in his *Frühe Gedichte*, when he reduced poetry to the expression of an emotion—' Sehnsucht ' :

> Ich möchte werden wie die ganz Geheimen :
> nicht auf der Stirne die Gedanken denken,
> nur eine Sehnsucht reichen in den Reimen. . . .

In place of this Rilke now offered something quite different, the patient, passive, absorbing state of the æsthete, who waits for impressions to come to him, collects them, ponders them, until " in a most rare hour the first word of a poem arises in their

midst and goes forth from them." This doctrine
is the very gospel of Æstheticism. It recalls some
famous sentences in Pater's *Renaissance* and, in the
use which it ascribes to the memory as a factor in
artistic creation, it bears some resemblance to the
view of art which Proust put forward in *Le Temps
Retrouvé*. But the mere collection of impressions
and sensations was not all that Rilke demanded.
They must be reduced to order and turned into a
work of art. To describe this process he found
a figure which fitted his ideas—the medieval stone-
mason who turned his feelings into the permanent
shape of the stone cathedral. In other words, the
poet's many experiences must be transmuted into
something independent and complete, something
which stands in its own right and needs for its
understanding no reference to the poet's life and
thought and feelings.

At first sight this doctrine might seem to bear a
close resemblance to that of the Parnassians. They
had not aimed, like Victor Hugo, at creating a
poetic personality whose every poem was but an
incident in a single career and intelligible largely
through what had preceded it. They had aimed
rather at creating single poems which stood by
themselves and needed neither preface nor comment.
In poems like Leconte de Lisle's *Les Eléphants*

there is no philosophy, no moralising, no personal revelation. It describes an occasion, an event; its appeal is entirely to the inner eye ; it says nothing to the heart or to the conscience. It exists by virtue of its vivid details and the design to which these are subordinated. It comments neither on the universe nor on the poet. But independence of this kind was not what Rilke achieved, nor what he wanted. His poems were much more than pictures in words ; much more went to their making than what he had merely seen. However independent he wanted his poetry to be, its independence would not be of the impersonal, pictorial, Parnassian kind. He started with an act of faith that every experience would ultimately become part of himself and that out of this enriched and complex self his poetry would emerge. But he also felt that when his poetry came, it would not be personal and subjective like his own earlier work but self-sufficient and complete in itself like a masterpiece of the visual arts.

Rilke's theory, then, might be regarded as an attempt to harmonise and combine two different views of poetry. On the one hand it demanded the fullness which comes from living in the imagination, from yielding to every impression, and in this it recalls the Romantics with their eager quest of sensations and their belief in the unique nature of the poet's calling. On the other hand it recalls Mallarmé's conception of the ideal poem as something absolute in itself and free from anything that might be called the private tastes of its maker. The two views are not easily reconciled; for the one asserts the importance of everything that the poet feels, the other demands that the poet's individuality must be omitted from the actual poem, which exists in its own world of pure art. But Rilke's attempt to combine the two views is intelligible in the light both of his time and of his own development. He saw, as others saw, that the Romantic personality was in many ways destructive to poetry, while the impersonal art of the Parnassians omitted too much. And in his own experience he had both known the ardours of an intense inner life and felt the majesty of works of art which were somehow complete in themselves. In his last years he turned again to the poetry of self-revelation, but before that he went through a time when he deliberately tried to lose himself in impressions, hoping that out of them he would create an objective and self-sufficient art.

In this task Rilke was helped by his temperament. He had a most unusual, almost an incomparable sensibility. He was often overwhelmed by experi-

ences. A casual sight might occupy his mind and
dominate his memory to the exclusion of other
experiences which common opinion might consider
more important and more attractive. He knew,
as few have known, the state of pure receptivity,
the true æsthetic condition, and when something
was given to him on these terms, it stayed with
him until it became a part of himself. From such
moments he made his poetry, and naturally he
sought them of his own choice, expecting new
excitements to come to him and deriving a strange
strength from them when they came. In his
search for them he looked all about him, in the
life of large towns such as Paris, in the monuments
of the past, in the unfamiliar sights of foreign
places, in sculpture and painting and architecture.
He passed much of his life in solitude that his
impressions might not be sullied or shaken by the
impacts of personal relations or the stress of living.
He regarded his æsthetic task as all-important, and
faced it with unrelaxed determination and self-
denial. In his search for beauty he was extremely
hard on himself. For it and through it he lived
and worked.

An attitude of this kind is unusual in a poet.
It might even be thought impossible. The creative faculty is usually accompanied by a strong

sense of independence and refuses to wait for
events to dictate to it.   Even those who live on
their emotions do not expect their emotions to be
imposed upon them from without.   But Rilke
was a true child and apostle of the Æsthetic Movement.   Where others have found a unifying
principle for themselves in religion or morality
or the search for truth, Rilke found his in the
search for impressions and the hope that these
could be turned into poetry.   To this task he
gave his religious fervour, his moral earnestness,
his intellectual integrity.   For him Art was what
mattered most in life.   But because of this he was
placed in a difficulty.   A poet may have a supreme
belief in the importance of Art, but he can hardly
find in it the source of his inspiration.   Mallarmé's
failure to write his perfect poem was largely the
result of his belief that somehow the pure æsthetic
experience, divorced from its irrelevant mani-
festations, was all that mattered to the poet.   And
even when a poet is not concerned with the
Beautiful as such, but contents himself with
absorption in individual works of art, his task is
not easy.   It is difficult to write poetry about
other poems, and only less difficult to write about
pictures and statues.   In all such work we feel
that there is inevitably something second-hand :

it seems to have no independent vision of life and to add nothing really new to our experience. But Rilke felt no such doubts. His concern with the arts was so serious and so single-minded that he tried to recapture through æsthetic appreciation the power and the vision which had gone to the making of masterpieces. The extraordinary thing is that he succeeded and found sources of original poetry in the works of other men.

Many of the poems in the *Neue Gedichte* are concerned with works of art. They vary greatly both in manner and in quality, and, on the whole, it seems true to say that the more Rilke liberates himself from a purely appreciative state, the more original and striking his work is. So long as his poetry is dominated simply by the impression which a masterpiece has made on him, he is more of a critic than a poet. He is able to convey this impression and to make us feel that what he sees is indeed worth seeing, but his poem is still second-hand. It is still the inspiring masterpiece that matters. This is true even of poems like *Früher Apollo* and *Die Fensterrose,* which are far from being merely descriptive. In both of them the object seen is still so important that Rilke can only weave fancies round it and praise it. His poem is a criticism, a commentary. But it is little more.

The window and the statue remain vastly more important than what is said about them. Sometimes this subordinate attitude degenerates into something that is hardly even poetry and is infused not with æsthetic pleasure, but with the dry light of historical interest or simply with a feeling for the quaint. In *Der König von Münster* and *Der aussätzige König*, for instance, Rilke has taken old tales which might have a human as well as a picturesque interest, but he presents them almost as oddities, and leaves them at that. Even in *Auferstehung* his feelings are set in a very minor key and hardly amount to more than a mild pleasure in the curious. In such cases Rilke's æsthetic pleasure in his subject was not strong enough to inspire poetry. He remained the mere æsthete.

Such failures are, however, not really to be attributed to Rilke's æstheticism. In them he is not the true lover of the beautiful but the sightseer, the man who is interested by the unusual but remains at a distance from it. He has failed to lose himself in what he sees or to gather the essential experience which it has to offer. But in practice the more Rilke lost himself in æsthetic contemplation, the more in the end he found for himself. When a sight ravished his senses and occupied his

G

mind, he came somehow to have a new vision of
what lay behind it, and from this he made poetry.
The process and its results may be illustrated from
Eva, written on a medieval statue of Eve. The
first half of the poem is almost purely appreciative.
The beauty of the statue has caught Rilke, and he
describes what he sees :

> Einfach steht sie an der Kathedrale
> grossem Aufstieg, nah der Fensterrose,
> mit dem Apfel in der Apfelpose,
> schuldlos-schuldig ein für alle Male
>
> an dem Wachsenden, das sie gebar,
> seit sie aus dem Kreis der Ewigkeiten
> liebend fortging, um sich durchzustreiten
> durch die Erde, wie ein junges Jahr.

So far he appeals to the eye. The stance and the
look of Eve have passed into his words. He sees
her as he imagines that the sculptor saw her. But
the second half of the poem deepens and widens its
meaning :

> Ach, sie hätte gern in jenem Land
> noch ein wenig weilen mögen, achtend
> auf der Tiere Eintracht und Verstand.
>
> Doch da sie den Mann entschlossen fand,
> ging sie mit ihm, nach dem Tode trachtend,
> und sie hatte Gott noch kaum gekannt.

In this Rilke has passed beyond his delighted enjoyment of the statue to an appreciation of the beliefs and feelings which inspired its sculptor. By entering into this medieval world and understanding it as a poet can, he has made Eve more human and more tender. She has become through his interpretation a symbol of certain innocent and charming qualities, a type of motherhood and wifehood, who by her devotion and pathos has a claim on our affections. Such she was for the Middle Ages ; so Rilke has seen her and presented her.

The experience captured in this way need not, of course, be historically correct. Towards history the poet has no obligations. Nor was Rilke always so respectful of the ideas of the past as he was in *Eva*. Indeed more usually he looked at a work of art from a peculiarly personal standpoint and found new meanings in themes which had been largely fixed by the conventions of centuries. The great events of the Gospels are a dangerous subject for any poet. Hallowed by the long tradition of Christian art they might seem unsuitable for Rilke, who had ceased to believe in their accepted sanctity. But both in *Der Ölbaumgarten* and in *Pietà* he extracted a new kind of pathos from the most tragic episodes of the old story. In both, too, his inspiration is not to be found in the plain words of

the Gospel but in the tradition created round them
by Italian painters. The hopeless despair of his
Christ on the Mount of Olives belongs more to
Mantegna than to St John. He is a purely human
figure, abandoned and miserable, and He turns
with His complaint to God:

> Ich finde Dich nicht mehr.   Nicht in mir, nein.
> Nicht in den andern.   Nicht in diesem Stein.
> Ich finde Dich nicht mehr.   Ich bin allein.
>
> Ich bin allein mit aller Menschen Gram,
> den ich durch Dich zu lindern unternahm,
> der Du nicht bist.   O namenlose Scham. . . .

The quivering pathos, the bitter complaint of these
lines, are not so grand as the few words of the
Gospel, but they are real and true. Rilke's Christ
is like all those who have attempted a splendid
task and found themselves betrayed and abandoned.
In *Pietà* also Rilke found his inspiration in Italian
art. The washing of the dead body of Christ by
the women who had loved Him was a theme which
drew from Titian and Michaelangelo some of their
noblest work, and into their vision of this scene
they inevitably brought a sense of tragic longing
for the dead which they depicted in the sorrow-
stricken figures of the Virgin and the Magdalene.

It is this which Rilke takes and makes the centre
of his poem. His Magdalene speaks in the language
of passionate desire, and the climax of the poem
comes when she says :

> Nun bist du müde, und dein müder Mund
> hat keine Lust zu meinem wehen Munde—.
> O Jesus, Jesus, wann war unsre Stunde ?
> Wie gehn wir beide wunderlich zugrund.

What moves Rilke in the story is the element of
frustrated love, and in this he finds a deeply moving
pathos. By concentrating on this he makes his
poem a new thing, although its subject is ancient
and familiar.   He does what the painters had done
in pictures but no poet had quite done before him.
So his art ceases to be derivative in any derogatory
sense.

   In other poems on similar subjects Rilke left his
sources, even the painters, behind and recreated
old stories in the light of his own convictions.
These convictions are not obtruded dogmatically,
nor are the poems meant to teach. They give
Rilke's views on some vital problems. He saw,
for instance, the story of the Prodigal Son as an
illustration of a difficulty which he had himself
felt deeply.   It is this which gives so strange a
power to *Der Auszug des verlorenen Sohnes*. In this

poem Rilke gives quite a new meaning to the
parable. He presents his own view in prose in
Malte Laurids Brigge, where he sees the story as
" the legend of one who did not want to be loved."
In the poem he gives the emotional and imaginative
content of this idea and depicts the man who wishes
at all costs to free himself from the potent bonds
of familiar life, to find a new existence far away from
all that he knows :

> Aus Drang, aus Artung,
> aus Ungeduld, aus dunkeler Erwartung,
> aus Unverständlichkeit und Unverstand :
> Dies alles auf sich nehmen und vergebens
> vielleicht Gehaltnes fallen lassen, um
> allein zu sterben, wissend nicht warum—
>
> Ist das der Eingang eines neuen Lebens ?

The poem gives an entirely new meaning to the
parable. The significance which Rilke has discovered is certainly not what many would discover
in the Bible story. And he finds it because his own
intense desire to escape determines his interpretation of the story. The Prodigal Son has become
a symbol to him. A similar transformation may
be seen in *Der Auferstandene*. There the familiar
theme of the Resurrection is seen from a new angle.
Through it runs the idea of ' love without the

beloved.' Rilke sees the Magdalene as one who is made by the Crucifixion to love Christ without wishing to be loved in return, and he marks the contrast between her appearances at the foot of the Cross and after the Resurrection :

> Sie begriff es erst in ihrer Höhle,
> wie er ihr, gestärkt durch seinen Tod,
> endlich das Erleichternde der Öle
> und des Rührens Vorgefühl verbot,
>
> um aus ihr die Liebende zu formen,
> die sich nicht mehr zum Geliebten neigt,
> weil sie, hingerissen von enormen
> Stürmen, seine Stimme übersteigt.

The idea which underlies this poem is more un-usual than that of the Prodigal Son, but it is not less true and not less moving. And it is Rilke's own. Through deep, impassioned meditation on an old story he has found the means to present one of his most fundamental ideas.

In his Prodigal Son and his Magdalene Rilke created symbolic figures for his own conceptions. In them he presents particular cases of universal problems which concerned him, and his poetry gains immensely by his peculiarly personal treat-ment and outlook. A similar process may be seen in his poems on contemporary subjects. He followed the dictates of his sensibility and wrote about whatever touched or moved him. Sometimes he was struck by quite trivial sights which could never be exalted into great poetry. In poems, for instance, like *Die Flamingos* and *Persisches Heliotrop* he appeals only to the eye. Such subjects might have been treated splendidly by the Impressionist painters ; they might even have inspired Heredia to sonorous and glittering lines. But they were not ideally suited to Rilke's gifts. He failed to catch the play of light and colour which is their chief claim. But such failures are exceptional. His sensibility was much more than of the eye. Certain sights awoke in him a deep feeling of pity, from which he could escape only by transforming his emotion into poetry. The things which so moved him were not always the common objects of pity, but sometimes what he saw affected him so vividly that it seemed to contain all the pathos in the world. In a caged panther, a revolving merry-go-round, a bachelor sitting alone in a room, a woman going blind, an old woman who had had a glorious moment of success in youth, he saw something at once enthralling and extremely painful. In this respect he resembled Thomas Hardy, who felt a similar overmastering pathos in a blinded bird or a diseased

man or a giant led by a dwarf at a fair. But for
Hardy, who was half a philosopher, these sights
were instances of a general disorder and cruelty of
the universe. From them he drew philosophical
conclusions and sometimes pointed a moral. But
for Rilke they indicated nothing metaphysical.
They are what he feels them to be, although his
feelings are not stated directly but through the
selection of details which make a composite picture. In *Der Panther* he writes about a caged
panther, but though there is no direct appeal for
sympathy, the poem is almost an assault on the
emotions :

> Sein Blick ist vom Vorübergehn der Stäbe
> so müd geworden, dass er nichts mehr hält.
> Ihm ist, als ob es tausend Stäbe gäbe
> und hinter tausend Stäben keine Welt.

Rilke's first emotion about the caged panther is
not unlike that which inspired Hardy to write *The
Blinded Bird*, but whereas Hardy breaks into impassioned denunciation of the order which allows
such things to be, Rilke passes no judgment and
closes his poem with an account of the panther
opening his eyes and seeing something which
transfixes his whole frame. He describes the
animal as it paces to and fro in its cage, and his
words are full of the minute and loving attention

of one who has felt the deep pathos of a strong
beast reduced to impotence. But all else is left
unsaid. We may draw conclusions as we like.
The poet states the facts as he has seen and felt
them, but he does not think it necessary to point
a moral.

The same method may be seen in another masterpiece, *Das Karussell*. It describes a merry-go-round
with its painted animals and the living children who
ride on them. The beginning is gay and happy ;
then Rilke continues :

> Und das geht hin und eilt sich, dass es endet,
> und kreist und dreht sich nur und hat kein Ziel.
> Ein Rot, ein Grün, ein Grau vorbeigesendet,
> ein kleines kaum begonnenes Profil.
> Und manchesmal ein Lächeln, hergewendet,
> ein seliges, das blendet und verschwendet
> an dieses atemlose blinde Spiel.

It is impossible to read this without feeling that
the merry-go-round with its mechanical rhythm, its
purposelessness, its innocent happy riders, is an
emblem of life. But of this Rilke says nothing,
and there is no warrant for assuming that he intended it. It might indeed be truer to say that he
makes the merry-go-round significant by attribut-
ing to it qualities which are sometimes attributed
to life. His poem is transparently clear ; it needs

neither addition nor explanation. But it produces
its effect largely because of the associations of
thought which it awakens and the richness which
its details have for the reader.

In *Der Panther* and *Das Karussell* Rilke kept his
own personality in abeyance. He did not even
interpret what he saw in the light of his own
dominant ideas. But even in them he used as a
background certain ideas which he later made
explicit in the *Duineser Elegien*. There the wild
animal is the type of self-contained life ; the Saltim-
banque, tossing on his carpet, is the type of purpose-
less activity. But such ideas he does not state
explicitly when writing of the panther and the
merry-go-round, and the poems are complete without them. In other poems of the *Neue Gedichte* he
develops certain ideas, and notably his ideas about
death. With these he was much occupied and,
though he never combined them into a doctrine,
they form a coherent whole whose parts appear in
different poems. The result is that when Rilke
writes about death, his work is curiously exciting
and mysterious. In *Der Tod des Dichters* he sees
the dead poet as one who returns to physical nature
and shows his oneness with it in his face :

> Die, so ihn leben sahen, wussten nicht,
> wie sehr er *eines* war mit allem diesen,

> denn dieses : diese Tiefen, diese Wiesen
> und diese Wasser waren sein Gesicht.

In *Todeserfahrung* he contrasts the uncertainty of our
lives here with the reality of the life beyond :

> Doch als du gingst, da brach in diese Bühne
> ein Streifen Wirklichkeit durch jenen Spalt,
> durch den du hingingst : Grün wirklicher Grüne,
> wirklicher Sonnenschein, wirklicher Wald.

This is almost philosophical poetry. Rilke presents a view of life and death which he assumes
to be true for all. But he presents it as a personal
question through vivid, particular images. His
æsthetic taste and discernment give force and detail
to his dominating idea.

The same idea underlies one of Rilke's finest
poems, *Orpheus. Eurydike. Hermes.* This was inspired by a Greek group in bronze at Naples, and
treats of an ancient myth by which the Greeks and
Romans symbolised the impassable gulf that lies
between the living and the dead. The sweet singer,
Orpheus, almost succeeds in bringing his wife up
from the realm of the dead, but when, overcome by
longing, he turns to look at her, he loses her for
ever. In this tragic story the Greeks symbolised
how song may almost recall the dead but cannot

allow us to see them face to face. Rilke, however, was not concerned with the usual interpretations of the myth. He did not, like Virgil, emphasise the appalling sense of loss which his mistake brought to Orpheus, nor, as Valery Bryusov has done in modern times, did he dwell on the heart-rending pathos of Orpheus' impatience. He saw the myth in the light of his own views of death. For him the dead have passed into the earth and become a part of the life-giving process which comes from it. Therefore for him the pathos and the power of the story are that Eurydice is no longer a woman but something deeply rooted in the nature of things. So when Orpheus turns round, she fails to recognise him :

> Sie war schon nicht mehr diese blonde Frau,
> die in des Dichters Liedern manchmal anklang,
> nicht mehr des breiten Bettes Duft und Eiland
> und jenes Mannes Eigentum nicht mehr.
> Sie war schon aufgelöst wie langes Haar
> und hingegeben wie gefallner Regen
> und ausgeteilt wie hundertfacher Vorrat.
>
> Sie war schon Wurzel.
> Und als plötzlich jäh
> der Gott sie anhielt und mit Schmerz im Ausruf
> die Worte sprach : Er hat sich umgewendet—,
> begriff sie nichts und sagte leise : Wer ?

The old story has been completely transformed by
the interpretation which Rilke gives to it.

In his æsthetic life, then, Rilke not merely found
subjects for poetry but was able to find himself
through these subjects and to create new and intensely personal poems in which an old idea was
transmuted through his vision of it. Thus he
succeeded in both parts of the task which he set
himself. His poems were certainly not 'emotions'
but 'experiences,' and they had that independence
and completeness which he saw symbolised in the
stone cathedral. No one else could have written
them, and on them all is the unmistakable imprint
of his workmanship. But as poems they stand by
themselves and need no explanation. Even when
he presents his original ideas, as in *Todeserfahrung*
or *Kindheit*, he presents them as strictly personal
matters, concerned with a particular occasion and
expressed through a remarkably individual choice
of images. Subjects of universal import are conveyed through his own special experience of them.
Here again he may be compared to Hardy, who
had a similar sensibility and similar originality of
mind. But Hardy could not, or would not, con-
fine himself to particular issues and special cases.
A single sight might prompt him to raise far-
reaching questions and to give answers which con-

cerned the whole nature of the universe. So, for instance, in *Nature's Questioning* the sight of water and fields and flocks at dawn suggests to him various explanations of the imperfection of life, and *The Bedridden Peasant* becomes a text for a discourse on the injustice of God. But Rilke never drew such lessons. If he had an idea to present, he presented it as a vivid experience of his own and left it at that, and more often his ideas are the implicit and unstated structure on which he shapes a poem. This is true even of such a poem as *Archaïscher Torso Apollos*, where the sight of a Greek statue makes a directly ethical appeal to him, and he closes with the words:

Sonst stünde dieser Stein entstellt und kurz
unter der Schultern durchsichtigem Sturz
und flimmerte nicht so wie Raubtierfelle

und bräche nicht aus allen seinen Rändern
aus wie ein Stern : denn da ist keine Stelle,
die dich nicht sieht. Du musst dein Leben ändern.

In spite of the final exhortation this is not didactic. The poem must be taken as a whole, and then it is seen to be an account of a special experience; the radiant beauty of the statue so moves the poet that he feels he must begin a new life. It is his own experience which he gives, and others may accept it or reject it as they choose.

The fact that Rilke wrote in accordance with his announced aims does not of course account for the whole of his success in the *Neue Gedichte*. "Poetry," it has been said, "is made with words," and in his management of words Rilke here shows a great advance on his earlier work. The free and easy rhythms of the *Frühe Gedichte* have given place to others in which the effect must be made in a small compass, and the variation comes less from the different swing of successive lines than from the pauses and changing movement of a single line. The rhythm has become an integral part of the whole and changes in sympathy with the poet's mood. Writing, for instance, about the martyr-dom of St. Sebastian he conveys through his rhythm the flight of the arrows and the unmoved stance of the martyr:

> Und die Pfeile kommen : jetzt und jetzt
> und als sprängen sie aus seinen Lenden,
> eisern bebend mit den freien Enden.
> Doch er lächelt dunkel, unverletzt.

The arrangement of the words and of the lines marks the contrast between the moving arrows and the unmoved saint. The same art may be

seen in the first stanza of *Die Erblindende*, where
the quiet pace of the words and the short phrases
of the fourth line convey the effect of a painful
truth slowly dawning during an occasion which
had seemed quite ordinary:

> Sie sass so wie die anderen beim Tee.
> Mir war zuerst, als ob sie ihre Tasse
> ein wenig anders als die andern fasse.
> Sie lächelte einmal. Es tat fast weh.

Then in the last verse the poet catches the woman's
hesitating, uncertain movements, which are not at
all like common walking:

> Sie folgte langsam, und sie brauchte lang,
> als wäre etwas noch nicht überstiegen;
> und doch: als ob, nach einem Übergang,
> sie nicht mehr gehen würde, sondern fliegen.

The common, everyday words fall exactly into the
rhythm which suits their subject. Rilke was so
great a master of his technique that he was able
to use only those words which exactly fitted his
purpose and conveyed, simply by their rhythm,
the shock of surprise which he felt in a commonplace setting at the realisation that a woman was
going blind.

In his æsthetic life Rilke collected experiences

H

and let them lie dormant in his mind until some chance occasion summoned them to the conscious surface and inspired him to make use of them. By this process he was able to make his poetry intensely suggestive and full of associations. This richness may be seen to great advantage in his similes, in which no modern poet has equalled him. Small and trivial things, which he had noticed and which are in themselves insufficient to make a poem, become vitally important when attached to some larger theme. So he describes Orpheus' gaze as he walks in front of Eurydice :

> der Blick ihm wie ein Hund vorauslief,
> umkehrte, kam und immer wieder weit
> und wartend an der nächsten Wendung stand.

Or Abishag, virginal and remote, bending over the old David at night :

> Sein wirres Leben lag
> verlassen wie verrufne Meeresküste
> unter dem Sternbild ihrer stillen Brüste.

Or an old Sibyl, whose age has passed reckoning as she stands in her place :

> schwarz wie eine alte Zitadelle
> hoch und hohl und ausgebrannt.

Or a blind man in Paris:

> Sieh, er geht und unterbricht die Stadt,
> die nicht ist auf seiner dunkeln Stelle,
> wie ein dunkler Sprung durch eine helle
> Tasse geht.

Or St. Sebastian at his martyrdom:

> Weit entrückt wie Mütter, wenn sie stillen,
> und in sich gebunden wie ein Kranz.

These similes are more than charming in themselves, more than right in their place. They are not mere decoration, nor, strictly speaking, decoration at all. They are vital to the poems in which they appear; for through them Rilke conveys shades of meaning essential to his design, for which plain statement is not enough. The nervous, forward-darting glance of Abishag, the ruinous weather-worn Sibyl, the impervious isolation of the blind man, the self-absorbed sanctity of St Sebastian, have each their own special individuality for the poet who has seen them as complex wholes, and to convey this he must use imagery. By his similes Rilke makes his poems far fuller and truer. They bring out the associations which his subjects have for him, and suggest hidden depths of meaning.

The similes would hardly be as successful as they are if Rilke had not set them in contexts where everything seems to be said in plain unassuming words.   Unlike some other poets of his generation, such as Stefan George and Gabriele d'Annunzio, Rilke uses a very simple vocabulary. He avoids recondite ' poetical ' words, and some of his finest effects are made through an apparent simplicity.   There is a complete lack not only of decoration, but even of any attempts at an elevated style, in lines such as

> Er wusste nur vom Tod, was alle wissen :
> dass er uns nimmt und in das Stumme stösst.

Or
> Wie hab ich das gefühlt, was Abschied heisst.

Yet these lines are not bald or prosaic.   They have the direct, powerful utterance which seems to come straight from a strong emotion.   In their concentrated strength they prepare the reader to expect something important, and by their luminous clarity they place the essential elements of the poem before him.   Then, after beginning in this way, Rilke sometimes inserts a simile or some other more picturesque element which gives colour to the poem and eases the intense strain of its emotion. But the foundation of something clearly seen and deeply felt remains intact. So, in *Ein Frauen-schicksal*, Rilke tells of a woman who has had a glittering moment in the past, followed by a long and dreary life. He compares her to a goblet jealously preserved for years because a king has once drunk out of it ; then he returns to the facts and states quietly and inevitably :

> Da stand sie fremd wie eine Fortgeliehne
> und wurde einfach alt und wurde blind
> und war nicht kostbar und war niemals selten.

The careful, deliberate words bring home the cold horror of the situation as it really is. And because they are, after all, usual, common words, they make the situation perfectly real and natural. There is no question here of romanticism. This is a poetry of life.

Rilke's varied and rich effects were largely the reward of his patient æstheticism. But they would never have been granted to him if he had not already possessed a singularly receptive and sensitive temperament. His great gifts, however, had a weakness, not inevitable perhaps, yet to be expected. Despite his training among masterpieces and his unwavering devotion to the Beautiful, Rilke had not an absolutely impeccable taste. Sometimes he seems to allow a trivial or disagreeable

image to mar an otherwise noble conception. In
Klage um Jonathan, for instance, he gave his own
version of David's lament for Jonathan, and
breathed a new tenderness and softness into it.
But in speaking of the actual pang of bereavement
he says :

> denn da und da, an meinen scheusten Orten,
> bist du mir ausgerissen wie das Haar,
> das in den Achselhöhlen wächst.

The image of the hair pulled from the arm-pit is
both vaguely disgusting and quite inadequate to
the sense of loss which pervades the rest of the
poem.   It may have meant more to Rilke than to
us ; for his sensitiveness may have been more
shocked and shaken by such a deprivation than
ours is.   But it is hard not to believe that this
failure in taste is not due to his very sensibility.
Because of it he felt things much more strongly
than most men do, and he was liable to attach
significance to some facts which are by common
consent trivial.   But such failures can hardly be
counted against him.   They seldom occur, and the
remarkable fact remains that on the whole his
sensibility was healthy, secure and delightfully
sane.   His occasional slips recall the way in which
Keats' sensuous appreciation of life sometimes led

him into coarseness and sensuality. In neither case do the faults impair the total impression made by the poet's work.

In the *Neue Gedichte* Rilke not only opened up new subjects for poetry, but he found a secret beauty in many unrecognised subjects. He was not a modern poet in the sense that he found charm in the discords and paradoxes of modern life. But he kept a singularly open mind and explored the possibilities of many subjects which had not before been introduced into poetry. Because of his love of artistic objects he found much to admire and understand in subjects so different as the Cathedral at Chartres, San Marco at Venice, small Flemish towns and islands in the North Sea, statues of the Buddha and of Artemis, of Adam and of Apollo. Through works of art he found his way into the study of the past and wrote about the last Hapsburg King of Spain, the Hebrew prophets, the Doges and the Christian Fathers. But his study of these was always primarily that of one who looked to see what strangeness of charm or interest they might have for him. He savoured the relics of the past as if they were works of art, and when he placed them in his poetry, it was always for some permanent element which he found in them. Sometimes this might seem unimportant. At other times, as in

his poems on the Buddha or on the figures of the
Christian saga, he found something that in spite of
its apparent remoteness was singularly intimate and
modern.

Rilke in fact tried to widen the range of poetry,
to find undiscovered subjects which would show
how much closer poetry lay to the life of every
day than many of its practitioners assumed. In
this main task he was triumphantly successful.
In the *Neue Gedichte* he showed that in common
sights and in threadbare stories there lurked vast
possibilities for the poet who had the courage and
the insight to find them. He was always original,
even in his failures, and his particular combination
of gifts is without parallel in our times. No other
poet has been so careful, so touching, so sensitive,
so widely appreciative. He had a wonderful way
of investing apparently unimportant things with
a magic light, and to what he saw through his
receptive imagination he brought all the resources
of a richly stocked memory and a consummate
sense of the associative value of words. He lacked
Stefan George's moral splendour, but he had something which George never had, a tenderness and
a sensibility which made his verses throb with
emotion or seem to pierce with clairvoyant vision
to the heart of life. By his achievement he showed

that the cult of the Beautiful need not mean the destruction of personality nor the creation of a colourless, shapeless type of mind. By his earnest and hard-won appreciation of masterpieces he widened and strengthened his nature, and by finding material which illumined some of his most intimate ideas he emerged from his æsthetic discipline a far richer personality, ready for the great tasks of his last years.

THE *DUINESER ELEGIEN*

By E. L. STAHL

THE *DUINESER ELEGIEN*

WHEN Rilke had completed his *Duineser Elegien* in 1922, he announced the event to his friends in words that may seem to us strangely ostentatious for so unassuming a man. We must, however, realise that he considered them as a task entrusted to him and to be performed with obedient self - effacement. Rarely has a poet waited so patiently for the moment of utterance and schooled himself so zealously in the smallest details of life, in order adequately to comply with his 'Diktat.' Yet he did so with no pride and no desire to be remarked and honoured. It was an unselfish cult of the self, an impersonal self-dedication.

Although, therefore, the personal element abounds in the Elegies and Rilke's individual associations and reminiscences constantly obtrude themselves, the purpose which he pursued was an objective one. The greatness as well as the obscurity of the Elegies lies in this psychological complexity, in the success with which Rilke, as the result of a conscious effort, treated his own intimate desires and recollections objectively, almost as things apart.

The growth of this purpose in Rilke's work might be made the subject of an absorbing study. The tendency towards objectivity can be called the distinguishing feature of his development. He began largely as a poet in the Romantic manner whose aim was the expression of joy, sorrow and longing because they were his own. But he adhered to this early conception of his art for a brief period only, for his efforts were soon directed to the aim, which he achieved in the Elegies and in the *Sonette an Orpheus*, of comprehending in poetry the true meaning of life. In retreating from Romanticism, however, he did not seek refuge, like the earlier Romantics and like his contemporary Richard Schaukal, in established units and systems—church, family, nation—but embarked independently on an endeavour to discover the purpose of human existence. Acknowledging no ties, he was left alone with nature and her creatures, the world of man and his own profound emotions and desires. Inevitably, perhaps, he began his search by projecting his moods and desires into the world around and by creating symbolic figures, the highest and most universal of which was God. He 'created' his God and attributed to Him all those qualities of loneliness, poverty and darkness which he felt and accepted for himself. But he soon perceived that in this process of transference the subjective element outweighed the objective, and that though he had reached the furthest limits he had not really departed from his earlier stage of self-expression. He therefore began again and, becoming the disciple and the apprentice of Rodin, he produced his 'Dinggedichte' in which he fashioned reality, though not in the Naturalist manner. He 'created' objects by revealing their inmost and essential qualities. He even 'created' himself (in part at any rate) in the figure of Malte Laurids Brigge, with an almost harsh determination to remain detached. But once again he saw that he had not achieved his aim, for he had in this experiment, necessary though it had been, concentrated too much on visual experiences. He expresses this conviction in a poem entitled *Wendung*:

Denn des Anschauns, siehe, ist eine Grenze,
und die geschautere Welt
will in der Liebe gedeihn.
Werk des Gesichts ist getan,
tue nun Herzwerk
an den Bildern in dir, jenen gefangenen. Denn du
überwältigtest sie ; aber nun kennst du sie nicht.

He realised that he was as far removed from his goal as at the time when he had completed the *Stunden-Buch*, and he felt that his purpose could be achieved only when subjective utterance and objective statement intimately coalesced in a work that directly purported to treat of human life and destiny. The Duino Elegies are this work.

It would be wrong to conclude that Rilke was pursuing a didactic purpose in his poetry. He did not wish, nor did he think that it was possible, to bring a message that might help and comfort others. It is the poet's task, he maintained, to justify, not to relieve, suffering :

"Irrtum plötzlich von der Kunst zu verlangen, dass sie bessere, erziehe, helfe—sie tut nichts von alledem, sie rühmt."

This conception of the poet's duty explains the texture and the movement of the Elegies. They begin with lament, but end with praise. Rilke felt that accusation and lament, however deeply concerned with the most universal human distress, express a purely negative attitude and signify immaturity if they are not finally, without being annulled, elevated to praise. The poet must proceed from the expression of distress to eulogy of the world which has caused his distress. At the time

when he began to compose the Elegies, in 1912, he wrote :

"Ich bin gerade jetzt mehr als je im Einseitigen, die Klage hat vielfach überwogen, aber ich weiss, man darf die Klagesaiten nur dann so ausführlich gebrauchen, wenn man entschlossen ist, auf ihnen, mit ihren Mitteln, später auch den ganzen Jubel zu spielen, der hinter jedem Schweren, Schmerzhaften und Ertragenen anwächst und ohne den die Stimmen nicht vollzählig sind."

Rilke's fundamental attitude in poetry, as in life, was one of admiration :

"Meine Produktivität geht aus der unmittelbarsten Bewunderung des Lebens, aus dem täglichen unerschöpflichen Staunen vor ihm hervor."

But this was no easy assertion of faith. With his extreme sensibility he fully experienced both the inadequacies and the perfections of life, and for many years it was his constant endeavour to recognise that the distresses and the felicities of life, even death and life themselves, could not be separated from one another. It was his final conviction that they belong together, necessarily and intimately, and that they form what he variously called 'a Unity,' 'one Being' and 'the Whole.' The many delays to which the writing and the completion of the Elegies were subjected were due

I

to Rilke's search for this supreme truth and to his
inability for a long time to express it adequately,
though he had found it. Without it he was unable to pass beyond the limits of lament, for it
was his sense of the unity of all things which
allowed him to proclaim that which had hitherto
caused him distress. He explained after he had
completed the Elegies :

"Unser effort, mein ich, kann nur dahin gehen, die
Einheit von Leben und Tod vorauszusetzen, damit sie
sich uns nach und nach erweise. . . . Wer nicht der
Fürchterlichkeit des Lebens irgendwann, mit einem
endgültigen Entschlusse, zustimmt, ja ihr zujubelt, der
nimmt die unsäglichen Vollmächte unseres Daseins nie
in Besitz, der geht am Rande hin, der wird, wenn einmal
die Entscheidung fällt, weder ein Lebendiger noch ein
Toter gewesen sein. Die Identität von Furchtbarkeit
und Seligkeit zu erweisen . . . dies ist der wesentliche
Sinn und Begriff meiner beiden Bücher (*i.e.* the Elegies
and the Sonnets)."

Viewed in the light of this 'effort,' the Elegies
are the crowning achievement of Rilke's work ;
and in particular they appear as the completion of
his task when they are compared with *Die Aufzeichnungen des Malte Laurids Brigge*. In *Malte* he
had written an elegiac novel, the history, sub-
jectively told, of one who was doomed to de-

struction because he was incapable of doing more than recognising that life was distressing and man inadequate. In 1915, when his work on the Elegies had ceased almost entirely, Rilke defined the themes of his novel :

"Wie ist es möglich zu leben, wenn doch die Elemente dieses Lebens uns völlig unfasslich sind ? Wenn wir immerfort im Lieben unzulänglich, im Entschliessen unsicher und dem Tode gegenüber unfähig sind, wie ist es möglich dazusein ? "

The task which he set himself to perform in the Elegies was to answer this question.

In both works life, death and love are the predominant themes, but the accents are differently placed. At the time when Rilke was preoccupied with the continuation and completion of the Elegies, he would recommend *Malte* to those only who could read it ' against the grain.' The reason for such repeated warnings is to be found in Rilke's later attitude of eschewing lament purely as lament. His work on the Elegies was painfully retarded by his experiences in the War. More deeply than ever he was immersed in distress, personal, spiritual and cultural. He had almost approached the stage when he felt sufficiently mature to affirm and praise. But the War drove him back on himself and in the almost only notable poem which he wrote during that period, in *Fünf Gesänge August 1914*, we find him retracing his steps and moving from praise to lament. The first two cantos sing the praise of the war-god :

> Zum erstenmal seh ich dich aufstehn,
> hörengesagter, fernster, unglaublicher Kriegs-Gott.

and

> Heil mir, dass ich Ergriffene sehe.   Schon lange
> war uns das Schauspiel nicht wahr,
> und das erfundene Bild sprach nicht entscheidend
> uns an.

But the third canto begins :

> Seit drei Tagen, was ists ?   Sing ich wirklich das
>   Schrecknis,
> Wirklich den Gott, den ich als einen der frühern
> nur noch erinnernden Götter ferne bewundernd
>   geglaubt ?

and continues :

>   Ist er ein Wissender ?   *Kann*
> er ein Wissender sein, dieser reissende Gott ?
> Da er doch alles Gewusste zerstört.   Das lange, das
>   liebreich,
> unser vertraulich Gewusstes.   Nun liegen die Häuser
> nur noch wie Trümmer umher seines Tempels.

Lament exceeds praise, which is voiced only in stoic acceptance of incomprehensible fate :

Aber im Rühmen, o Freunde, rühmet den Schmerz
    auch,
rühmt ohne Wehleid den Schmerz, dass wir die
    Künftigen nicht
waren, sondern verwandter
allem Vergangenen noch : rühmt es und klagt.
Sei euch die Klage nicht schmählich. Klaget. Wahr
    erst
wird das unkenntliche, das
keinem begreifliche Schicksal,
wenn ihr es masslos beklagt und dennoch das masslos,
dieses beklagteste, seht : wie ersehntes begeht.

                              (Canto 4)

Such submissive acceptance of human distress is
retained as an element of Rilke's final affirmation,
which is expressed in praise. The Tenth Elegy
in particular contains his mature assertion that our
abode on earth is suffering, that sorrows are

    unser winterwähriges Laub, unser dunkeles Sinngrün,
    eine der Zeiten des heimlichen Jahres—, nicht nur
    Zeit—, sind Stelle, Siedelung, Lager, Boden, Wohnort.

But here it is only one element in a large sphere
of praise, whereas in the *Fünf Gesänge* it is the sole
component. In the *Fünf Gesänge* accusation and
lament are not fully merged in praise, human fate
is accepted rather than affirmed. Accusation and
lament are also here directed against a force which
transcends humanity. The destructive incursions

of this superior power make human fate incomprehensible and human inadequacy almost excusable.   Rilke's experiences in the War had diverted him from the path of his true enquiry, which was the search for the answer to the question : " How can we exist in the face of our inadequacies in life, death and love ? "

The refuge which he found in the Castle of Muzot in Switzerland permitted him to efface the effects of this interruption and to complete the work begun at Duino.   Here he was able to regain that clearness of vision and to acquire that measure of human self-esteem which allowed him to sound the theme of praise in the Elegies.   He was now able to define the true relation between life and death, and to recognise that despite our many inadequacies we are intended to perform a high and immortal task.   It was one of his purposes, he said, " das Leben gegen den Tod hin offen zu halten."   By accepting human sorrow and distress and, while not ceasing to lament the nature of man, vindicating his existence, he was able to carry out his resolve.

Rilke does not ask : " How shall we act, knowing ourselves to be inadequate in life, love and death ? "   His question is not an ethical one, even as his poetry is not meant to be didactic.   Rather he considers the ultimate and metaphysical reasons for human existence : " How can we exist ? "   In the *First Elegy* the question is put in different words : " Whom can we use ? "   Actually it is the same query, since the justification for our existence is implicated in the ability, which we may or may not possess, to use and be useful to other creatures and things.

Rilke, asserting our inadequacy, begins the theme of lament : " Whom can we use ? "

> Engel nicht, Menschen nicht,
> und die findigen Tiere merken es schon,
> dass wir nicht sehr verlässlich zu Haus sind
> in der gedeuteten Welt.

We fail to respond, he continues, to the mute expectant appeal which, as he deeply felt, comes to us from the simple creatures and objects of the world, and he reproaches himself for neglecting his own poetic task, the carrying out of this mandate with an impersonal utterance :

> Aber bewältigtest du's ?   Warst du nicht immer
> noch von Erwartung zerstreut, als kündigte alles
> eine Geliebte dir an ?

This is a severe self-condemnation when we re-member the work which he had already done in the *Neue Gedichte*.   But he seems to have felt that his ' effort ' had, on the whole, not been sufficiently objective in the profoundest and most cogent sense.   One duty above all remained, to sing the praises of those women like Gaspara Stampa who, abandoned in love, free themselves of their lovers and yet continue to love.   They are for Rilke the representatives of life at its highest and purest, and their love can inspire others to emulation.   The full significance of their essentially ' open ' life can become clear only when he has developed his thoughts on this theme in the Eighth Elegy. They have their place in the First Elegy, because they supply in part an answer to Rilke's opening question.   We can ' use ' these lovers, who while loving disregard the object of their love, as a stimulus to higher aims.

We can also use, he continues, those who have died young, and for a brief time too we can be of use to them.   In order to understand these statements it is necessary to recall some features of Rilke's conception of death.

He believed that from the beginning of life death grows within us, and that death matures when life departs.   Our experiences and our achievements in life contribute to this process of ripening.   A certain span of life is therefore the necessary condition of our maturing for death.

In death new activities await us, for which our achievements in life prepare us. This belief is the central theme of Rilke's moving Requiem *Für eine Freundin*, which ends thus :

> Komm nicht zurück. Wenn du's erträgst, so sei
> tot bei den Toten. Tote sind beschäftigt.
> Doch hilf mir so, dass es dich nicht zerstreut,
> wie mir das Fernste manchmal hilft : in mir.

He expressed it also in a letter :

> " Wer weiss ob wir nicht in jenseitigen Verhältnissen irgendwie davon abhängen, dass wir hier zu dem Ende gekommen sind, das uns nun einmal bereitet war ; auch ist keine Sicherheit dafür gegeben, dass wir, aus zu grosser Mündigkeit von hier hinausflüchtend, drüben nicht vor neuen Leistungen stehen, vor denen sich die Seele, bestürzt und unberufen wie sie ankäme, erst recht beschämt fände."

He further believed that there is no diminution of life in death, that our fullest existence is in death :

> " So wenig die Ruhe ein Abnehmen von Bewegung ist, vielmehr eine unermessliche Steigerung ins grössere weltischere Bewegt- und Hingerissensein (unter Verzicht auf willkürliche Eigenbewegung), so wenig ist der Tod eine Lebensverminderung oder ein Verlust an Leben ; es scheint mir sicher, dass wir unter diesem seltsamen Namen das völlige Leben meinen, die Vollzähligkeit des Lebens, alles Leben in Einem."

These two conceptions, that life and death form a unity and that death is the consummation of life, explain Rilke's terse and recondite thoughts concerning the youthful dead in the First Elegy. They are immature when they die, since their death had had no opportunity to ripen within them. For them therefore death is strange and their first experience in death is slow regain. But as life and death are one, we, the living, can be of use to them until finally they outgrow our aid and then it is we who have need of them :

> Und das Totsein ist mühsam
> und voller Nachholn, dass man allmählich ein wenig
> Ewigkeit spürt.—Aber Lebendige machen
> alle den Fehler, dass sie zu stark unterscheiden.
> Engel (sagt man) wüssten oft nicht, ob sie unter
> Lebenden gehn oder Toten.   Die ewige Strömung
> reisst durch beide Bereiche alle Alter
> immer mit sich fort und übertönt sie in beiden.

> Schliesslich brauchen sie uns nicht mehr, die Frühe-
> entrückten,
> man entwöhnt sich des Irdischen sanft, wie man den
> Brüsten
> milde der Mutter entwächst.   Aber wir, die so
> grosse
> Geheimnisse brauchen, denen aus Trauer so oft
> seliger Fortschritt entspringt—: *könnten* wir sein ohne
> sie ?

In the First Elegy we hear the principal themes of the work, which after this preliminary statement proceeds almost in the manner of a symphony. It will be found to contain the principles of repetition, development and solution, and even the general scheme of *Adagio* and *Presto* may be seen to correspond somewhat to Rilke's main movements of lament and praise.

But though the First Elegy foreshadows the scope of the whole work, and though an answer has been found for the question of human usefulness, there can be no doubt that as yet the theme of lament vastly predominates. No adequate justification of human existence has been given, and indeed the Elegies that follow pursue the examination of life and continue the theme of lament.

In the *Second Elegy* Rilke contrasts human nature with that of the angels. The angels are the perfect first creation of God, the pollen of the divine flower, infinitely luminous and real, tumultuously ecstatic yet always able to recapture and recreate their emotions :

> Pollen der blühenden Gottheit,
> Gelenke des Lichtes, Gänge, Treppen, Throne,
> Räume aus Wesen, Schilde aus Wonne, Tumulte
> stürmisch entzückten Gefühls und plötzlich, einzeln,

Spiegel, die die entströmte eigene Schönheit
wiederschöpfen zurück in das eigene Antlitz.

But we lack this power of infinite and recreative reality of feeling. We pass on from emotion
to emotion, growing dimmer within, exhausting
our fragrance. Neither our affections, nor our
beauty, nor even the simple expressions of our
faces have any permanence of being. For ourselves we have no testimony of perpetuity. Even
the lovers, who believe that their emotions will
endure, have no proofs and they too experience
mutability. What else can we therefore do but
deny ourselves the recreative ecstasies of the
angels and wisely refrain from supreme dedication
when we love and part ? Such restraint is pictured
on Attic gravestones, for the Greeks knew that it is
the gods who have the right to urge, not we. And
we to-day have not even the consolation, which the
Greeks had, of finding a true and limited human
field and of representing our exalted aspirations
in art.

It is seen that the Second Elegy instances two
reasons for lament, which must be distinguished,
for upon this twofold result depend the further
development of the Elegies and the final answer to
Rilke's question. First, the nature of man generally is at all times transient and evanescent.

Secondly, the life of man in the modern world suffers from the absence of valid external symbols for the inward actions of his soul. Rilke believed that there has been a decline in this sense since the age of Tasso : " Es wird immer schwerer, für das, was die Seele tut, die äussere Handlung zu finden." Since the sixteenth century, life has been retreating into invisible inward regions :

"Damals fing vielleicht das an, was wir schon so seltsam vollzogen um uns sehen, das Zurückschlagen einer im Äusseren überfüllten Welt ins Innere. Sie werden verstehen, was ich meine : die inneren Erlebnisse waren im sechzehnten Jahrhundert im Sichtbaren draussen zu einer solchen Herrlichkeit gediehen, dass sie weiter nicht zu steigern war."

We are now unable to create new objects of an intimately human value (for Rilke could not believe that our modern objects are the expression of a *new* soul), and the objects that have come down to us from past ages are doomed to irreparable destruction :

"Noch für unsere Grosseltern war ein 'Haus,' ein 'Brunnen,' ein ihnen vertrauter Turm, ja ihr eigenes Kleid, ihr Mantel : unendlich mehr, unendlich vertraulicher ; fast jedes Ding ein Gefäss, in dem sie Menschliches vorfanden und Menschliches hinzusparten. Nun drängen, von Amerika her, leere gleich-

gültige Dinge herüber, Schein-Dinge, Lebens-Atrappen
. . . Ein Haus, im amerikanischen Verstande, ein ameri-
kanischer Apfel oder eine dortige Rebe, hat *nichts*
gemeinsam mit dem Haus, der Frucht, der Traube, in
die Hoffnung und Nachdenklichkeit unserer Vorväter
eingegangen war. . . . Die belebten, die erlebten, die
uns mitwissenden Dinge gehen zur Neige und können
nicht mehr ersetzt werden."

The Second Elegy for the first time voices this
complaint, but it is left to the Seventh Elegy to
develop it more fully. The Second Elegy, also
for the first time, hints that the lovers share our
human imperfection. The woman who loves is,
nevertheless, a figure approaching perfection.
Compared with her, man is untutored and inadequate when he loves. He falls immeasurably
short of the achievements of woman in love. There
is no male counterpart, according to Rilke, to the
distinctive glory and pure essential love of women
like Gaspara Stampa, Louize Labé and Maria
Alcoforado : " Der Mann hat sich (die Heiligen
ausgenommen) seit der Antike überhaupt nicht in
die Liebe eingelassen." When a man loves, he
does so with his selfish instinct and his blood, and
he is the instrument of dark biological forces.
The *Third Elegy* laments this male inadequacy in
love. Neither mother nor maiden elicits the

tumults of blood, nor are they able to soothe and fully restrain it. Our love is not born of one year, like that of the flowers, it is the work of countless generations :

> Siehe, wir lieben nicht, wie die Blumen, aus einem
> einzigen Jahr ; uns steigt, wo wir lieben,
> unvordenklicher Saft in die Arme.

In the face of such overpowering primeval forces all that the maiden can do is to perform a trustworthy daily deed, to assure and perhaps restrain for a while.

In the *Fourth Elegy* the lament becomes more extended and profound. In language and imagery of unusual suggestiveness, but replete with esoteric meaning, Rilke passes judgment on human nature. No simpler words could convey his thought which, concerned with the limitations of human consciousness, must itself transgress the sphere of ordinary consciousness. Dealing with the inexpressible, it is intuitive rather than rational.

The Elegy begins by asserting that we have no common consciousness of death and that we are at the same time conscious of life and death :

> Blühn und verdorrn ist uns zugleich bewusst.

Our consciousness is never pure, never without an
'opposite.' For our every feeling, desire and
intention there exists, inevitably, something contrary. We are at home in enmity. Backgrounds of
contrast are our essentials. We cannot pursue
our feelings to their pure end ; from outside they
are restricted and corrupted until they become
matter-of-fact, like the life of a dancer which,
in reality, is a bourgeois affair. We are but un-
authentic masqueraders ('halbgefüllte Masken')
and it would be better if we could be puppets ; we
should then at least be decided beings, even though
we should dwell in a world bereft of ' human '
values, on a darkened, empty stage. And Rilke,
continuing in terms of his personal experience,
appeals to his father (who is dead, but still fears
for his son's fate and future) and to his friends,
who could never prevent his love from extending
beyond them into eternity. He appeals to them
to acknowledge that his belief is justified, that the
play of life would be better if we had been denied
even the limited measure of free-will which we
possess. For then the action would be proper, as
between angel and puppet, actor and acted. Then
the course of whatever happened could be run
completely and we, who by our very presence
disunite, should not be in the way any longer. In

the eyes of the dead our achievements can seem
little more than pretexts. Nothing in our lives is
truly genuine, except some hours in our childhood,
during which we are in contact with more than
the mere past and not concerned about the future.
Lacking adult consciousness, there is for us in
childhood no ' opposite' to disconcert us and we
are happily occupied with that which lasts and are
fit to take part in a pure event. The Elegy therefore ends in praise of the child, whose death, Rilke
says, has none of the beauty of maturing, but is as
ugly as bread that grows hard or as the core of an
apple, and yet does not make the child malicious
while depriving it of so much.

This Elegy is one of the most representative of
the series, expressing Rilke's profoundest aims and
desires. More than anything else he wished that
love, thought, feeling and action should be ' pure,'
that is, complete in themselves, unalloyed by any
consciousness of an ' opposite.' He terms that
love pure which is directed to no object, and he
found it in the lives of the nun Maria Alcoforado
and other women. Feeling and thought would be
similarly pure if we could do without objects for
them and attain to an activity which is simply an
event. But by our very nature we are made to
depend in our conscious life on ' determining '

K

factors, and it is this limitation which occasions Rilke's deepest lament.

Kant had defined the human situation with philosophic sobriety, and he may have derived some consolation from the acknowledgment of our finiteness. But for Rilke (as for Kleist, to whose essay on the marionette theatre this Elegy owes much) it becomes a matter of human despair. It is for this reason that both Rilke and Kleist, repudiating the value of all human freedom because it is but limited, proclaim the virtues of the puppet, which is an unambiguous being, untroubled by consciousness and decided in its nature. Rilke does not, as some interpreters think, introduce the puppet into the Elegies because it is the lowest form of existence. On the contrary, it is a foil to the inadequacy of human existence, a figure of contrast like the animal, the pure 'open' life of which will be glorified in the Eighth Elegy.

The *Fifth Elegy*, the last to be written, indirectly continues this train of thought. Rilke's praise had hitherto been elicited by two human figures only : the lover and the one who dies young. In a letter from Duino he explains :

"Ich habe kein Fenster auf die Menschen, endgültiger-weise. Sie geben sich mir nur soweit, als sie in mir selbst zu Worte kommen, und da teilen sie sich mir während dieser letzten Jahre fast nur aus zwei Gestalten mit, von denen aus ich im Grossen auf die Menschen zurückschliesse. Was zu mir vom Menschlichen redet, immens, mit einer Ruhe der Autorität, die mir das Gehör geräumig macht, das ist die Erscheinung der Jungverstorbenen und unbedingter noch, reiner, unerschöpflicher : *die Liebende.* In diesen beiden Figuren wird mir Menschliches ins Herz gemischt, ob ich will oder nicht. Sie treten in mir auf sowohl mit der Deutlichkeit der Marionette (die ein mit Überzeugung beauftragtes Äusseres ist), als auch als abgeschlossene Typen, über die es nicht mehr hinausgeht, so dass die Naturgeschichte ihrer Seele könnte geschrieben werden."

Later his interest was aroused by two additional human figures, and for no very dissimilar reasons : the acrobat and the hero. The former is the subject of the Fifth, the latter of the Sixth Elegy.

Stimulated by one of Picasso's pictures, Rilke in the Fifth Elegy describes the life of the acrobats as more than ordinarily human, more transient even than that of other men :

> Wer aber sind sie, sag mir, die Fahrenden, diese ein
>   wenig
> Flüchtigern noch als wir selbst, die dringend von
>   früh an
> wringt ein wem—wem zuliebe
> niemals zufriedener Wille ?

The fugacity of their existence has this particular quality, that it is nearly a 'pure event.' They are playthings in the hands of grief, which continually turns and twists them into the same postures. There is no joy in this spectacle, and the interest of the onlookers who surround them like the petals of a blowing rose can only be due to the fact that it awakens in them displeasure at their own fate. But that the actors themselves feel the pain of their vocation and are yet able to smile —this makes them worthy of praise even to the angel, so that their activity can become a model for us. In this world we may be material in the hands of death which, like a milliner, works us up into manifold ornaments for the cheap hats of fate. But beyond, there may be a place where lovers succeed in pure love. They would then be like the acrobats and we should be happy spectators.

The vocation of the acrobats, who as human beings are subject to the infirmities lamented in the Fourth Elegy, is a symbol for the 'pure' human activity envisaged in that Elegy. Their life is the nearest human approach to the existence of the puppet, and they are the model for the lovers. Fate impels them, and they seem to be its willing instruments.

The *Sixth Elegy* is devoted to the hero. He, too, is the instrument of fate :

das uns finster verschweigt, das plötzlich begeisterte
  Schicksal
singt ihn hinein in den Sturm seiner aufrauschenden
  Welt.

We tarry in life, preoccupied with the purpose of flowering, and betray our fruit, which is death. But the hero, urged on to the final goal, disregards life and bears his fruit, like the fig-tree, without flowering. And like the youthful dead he is little concerned to remain in the world. Life is only a beginning for him and even his episodes of love are but the stations of his progress. He can exist without being distracted by an ' opposite.'

But lest this should be thought to mean that life must be rejected as an unnecessary and disconcerting impediment on the path to death, the *Seventh Elegy* immediately proceeds to the glorification of existence. At the point when the value of human life in this world seems to have been completely denied, Rilke proclaims its virtues. Arriving at the furthest possibility of negation he affirms : " Hiersein ist herrlich." The tide of his poetry is on the turn from lament to praise.

In the First Elegy he had accused himself of
neglecting his poetic task :

> Aber bewältigtest du's ?   Warst du nicht immer
> noch von Erwartung zerstreut, als kündigte alles
> eine Geliebte dir an ?

Now his achievement seems assured, his utterance
has at last become profoundly impersonal. His
own development is complete and he has attained,
we might say, the 'pure' attitude of thinking
and feeling without envisaging the 'opposite,'
his beloved. His poetry is a 'pure' event, not a
plea directed towards a transcendent power. Rilke
expresses this attitude by saying that his voice has
outgrown its former purpose and that he desires
to 'solicit' no longer :

> Werbung nicht mehr, nicht Werbung, entwachsene
>   Stimme,
> sei deines Schreies Natur.

Not that his voice has no power of solicitation.
He could summon, he says, the invisible beloved
and make her respond, and his poetry could then
fully proclaim the beauties of spring and summer
with their times and seasons and stars. But the
summons would be heard by the many maidens
who have died, and the poet, conscious of his

task, would not be able to limit the scope of his call. They would come from their impotent graves that cannot retain them, to hear the message of one who has understood :

> Ihr Kinder, ein hiesig
> einmal ergriffenes Ding gälte für viele.

Their love was pure and they knew the glory of life—those even who were condemned to a life of privation and misery in sordid cities ; each of them had at least one hour, or perhaps an unmeasurable span, of full existence. For happiness, Rilke continues, is greatest when it is not visible, when it is an inward possession. Our real world is inward and invisible. We are, he continues, experiencing in our age the decline of that which is concrete and visible. Mental images are substituted for the permanent houses of other times. The creations of our age are stores of energy (triumphs of mechanical science) which are as shapeless as the wearing speed that we extract from everything. Our age knows temples no longer. But though our hearts thus go to waste, we are nevertheless inwardly building greater statues and pillars. At every turn the world has taken there have been such disinherited men as we now are, to whom neither the past nor the

future belonged.   This should not confuse us, but
should urge us to preserve those shapes which we
still appreciate.   For there they have stood, secure
amid uncertainty and fate.   And Rilke, addressing
the angel whom he now will not solicit, proclaims
to him the beauty of human creations and achievements, of cathedrals, music and love.

For the first time in the body of the Elegies
praise outweighs lament.   In some of the preced-
ing poems there had been eulogy.   But it had
concerned isolated members and individual representatives of humanity (the lovers, the prematurely
dead, the acrobats, the hero), never the race as a
whole.   Now we are all entitled to share the praise
which Rilke has to bestow.   Such regret as exists
is mainly occasioned not by inadequacy on our
part, but by the inevitable trend of history.   In
this Seventh Elegy, therefore, one of the two
laments voiced in the Second Elegy has been
answered.   Man in the modern world has no
meaner mission than his ancestors.   It is in truth
a greater task : to build invisibly that for which
they were able to find outward and visible images.

The path now seems clear for final praise, the
answer to the wider question concerning man
generally : " Why, being inadequate, should we
exist at all ? "   Rilke does not proceed to give this

answer immediately. In the *Eighth Elegy* he
returns to lament. This shows that lament is not
removed by praise, that even in the most affirmative
estimate of our human value the realisation of our
inadequacy subsists ; for in the Eighth Elegy the
theme of lament is sounded with no abatement of
poignancy.

Human nature is compared with that of the
animal. The animal, says Rilke, lives an ' open '
life ; it is not burdened with our consciousness of
an ' opposite.' Death is not its opponent. Death
lies behind it and it moves steadily towards God,
into pure space. It has an existence of pure
infinity untroubled by the task of self-compre-
hension :

Sein Sein ist ihm
unendlich, ungefasst und ohne Blick
auf seinen Zustand, rein, so wie sein Ausblick.
Und wo wir Zukunft sehn, dort sieht es alles
und sich in allem und geheilt für immer.

It is different with us. Rilke believed that we,
by the very nature of our existence, move ' behind '
God, though we are at one with Him. He expressed this thought in a letter :

" Wer weiss, ich frage mich, ob wir nicht immer sozu-
sagen an der Rückseite der Götter herantreten, von
ihrem erhaben strahlenden Gesicht durch nichts, als

durch sie selber getrennt, dem Ausdruck, den wir
ersehnen, ganz nah, nur eben hinter ihm stehend—aber
was will das anderes bedeuten, als dass unser Antlitz
und das göttliche Gesicht in die selbe Richtung hinaus-
schauen, einig sind ; und wie sollen wir demnach aus
dem Raum, den der Gott vor sich hat, auf ihn zutreten?''

Before us lies the world as an 'opposite,' and we
alone see death.   We are never in pure and un-
restricted space, the object of no control or
desire :
Immer ist es Welt
und niemals Nirgends ohne Nicht :
das Reine, Unüberwachte, das man atmet und
unendlich *weiss* und nicht begehrt.

Children have moments of pure existence : *we*
achieve it when we approach death and when we
are in death.   The lovers would possess it, were
it not for their partners in love.   But for us there
is no escape from our fate, the fate of those who
always *face* the world, who are forever the spectators of life.   During our lives we are always
taking leave of life :

Und wir : Zuschauer, immer, überall,
dem allen zugewandt und nie hinaus !
Uns überfüllts.   Wir ordnens.   Es zerfällt.
Wir ordnens wieder und zerfallen selbst.
Wer hat uns also umgedreht, dass wir,

was wir auch tun, in jener Haltung sind
von einem, welcher fortgeht ?   Wie er auf
dem letzten Hügel, der ihm ganz sein Tal
noch einmal zeigt, sich wendet, anhält, weilt—
so leben wir und nehmen immer Abschied.

But even the animals are not fully at home in
the world. They are sad with the memory of
another home, of the intimate and reassuring life
in the womb :

Hier ist alles Abstand,
und dort wars Atem.   Nach der ersten Heimat
ist ihm die zweite zwitterig und windig.

The greatest pain of life is departure from the
womb into the world, so that even birds and bats
are dismayed when they must leave their nests
and venture to fly.   Serenity of joy is known only
by those minute creatures which are bred not in a
womb, but on earth.   Rilke explains this thought
in a letter :

"Dass eine Menge Wesen, die aus draussen ausge-
setzten Samen hervorgehen, *das* zum Mutterleib haben,
diese weite erregbare Freie,—wie müssen sie ihr ganzes
Leben lang sich drin heimisch fühlen, sie tun ja nichts
als vor Freude hüpfen im Schoss ihrer Mutter wie der
kleine Johannes ; denn dieser selbe Raum hat sie ja
empfangen und ausgetragen, sie kommen gar nie aus
seiner Sicherheit hinaus.   Bis beim Vogel alles ein
wenig ängstlicher wird und vorsichtiger.   Sein Nest

ist schon ein kleiner, ihm von der Natur geborgter
Mutterschoss, den er nur zudeckt, statt ihn ganz zu
enthalten. Und auf einmal, als wäre es draussen nicht
mehr ganz sicher genug, flüchtet sich die wunderbare
Reifung ganz hinein ins Dunkel des Geschöpfs und
tritt erst in einer späteren Wendung zur Welt hervor,
sie als eine zweite nehmend und den Begebenheiten der
früheren, innigeren nie mehr ganz zu entwöhnen."

The singularity of Rilke's thought becomes evident when the substance of this Elegy is compared
with the common view.   Schiller, for example, in
his essay *Über Anmut und Würde* writes :

"Bei dem Tiere und der Pflanze gibt die Natur nicht
bloss die Bestimmung an, sondern führt sie auch allein
aus. Dem Menschen aber gibt sie bloss die Bestimmung und überlässt ihm selbst die Erfüllung derselben.
Dies allein macht ihn zum Menschen."

The idealistic conception of human destiny is
foreign to Rilke.   He believed that our existence
is not more dignified, but a little darker, than that
of other beings, and more evanescent, like the
smile of a wind.   Why then, he asks in the *Ninth
Elegy*, knowing the sadness of our lot, should we
not wish to depart from it ?

warum dann

Menschliches müssen—und, Schicksal vermeidend,
sich sehnen nach Schicksal ? . . .

The reply to this question is at last the answer to
Rilke's enquiry in the Elegies, the solution of his
problem. The query at the beginning of the Ninth
Elegy must be read in conjunction with that of the
First concerning the usefulness of human existence.
The purpose of our existence, he says, is not happiness or knowledge or experience. We exist because
existence is in itself of value and because everything
which exists apparently appeals to us and depends
on us for its future existence, though in this world
we are the most fleeting creatures of all. But we
pass on into another world, and it is our task to
ensure for other beings a form of continued existence. We accomplish this task by expressing their
hidden and inner meaning and by taking this possession 'across' with us. The purpose of our existence
is to praise and extol the simple things of existence.
Our powers do not rise to higher things ; our
experiences, the events of this world, our pain,
unhappiness and love are all unutterable and they
are unrequired testimony in the beyond :

> Bringt doch der Wanderer auch vom Hange des
>   Bergrands
> nicht eine Hand voll Erde ins Tal, die allen unsägliche,
>   sondern
> ein erworbenes Wort, reines, den gelben und blaun
> Enzian.

Rilke now knows that love, even with its disappointments, is a mission entrusted to the lovers by the earth for the joy of all things. He knows too that precisely because those simple things which we are able to appreciate are doomed to disappear (Seventh Elegy), it is our task to extol them. Amid the forces of destruction our heart subsists:

> Zwischen den Hämmern besteht
> unser Herz, wie die Zunge
> zwischen den Zähnen, die doch,
> dennoch die preisende bleibt.

Compared with the angel we are deficient in feeling (*cf.* Second Elegy), but we can show him and praise to him the simple things of this world. We can save them from decay and give them a measure of permanence by making them an inward and invisible part of ourselves:

> Und diese, von Hingang
> lebenden Dinge verstehn, dass du sie rühmst; vergänglich,
> traun sie ein Rettendes uns, den Vergänglichsten, zu.
> Wollen, wir sollen sie ganz im unsichtbarn Herzen verwandeln
> in—o unendlich—in uns! wer wir am Ende auch seien.

We have received from the earth, Rilke says, a mandate to make her invisible within us, and he accepts the mission, which is above all a poet's vocation, and extols it in verses of moving simplicity and directness.

The existence of man is justified. He has a purpose in life which is not invalidated by his many inadequacies; he has an immortalising mission, and he can, after all, enter death and meet the approving angels. With this affirmation of life achieved, Rilke is now entitled to say, in the *Tenth Elegy*, that pain and sorrow are not a passing season of our life, to be sped and curtailed, but our permanent abode in life and death. We do not enter a land of happiness in death, and we should not spend our life, as we do, in a perpetual effort to appease and mitigate our distress. The principle of the whole of our life, in this world and the next, is sorrow.

To convey these concluding thoughts, Rilke employs an allegory of suffering which fills the Tenth Elegy. He contrasts life and death as the City and the Land of Pain. In life we do all we can to remove and conceal sorrow. We have arranged our life like a noisy fair to distract us from death and to reward those who are a little more skilful than others. It is only the children,

the lovers and the animals who have no share in
this shallow gaiety. For a short while in their
lives young men too follow a Lament (personified
as a female figure) into the country beyond. But
soon they desert her and return to the scene of
frolic. Only those who die young, in that stage
of death which weans them from life, consort
with her lovingly. Then, on their journey into
death, they are received by an older Lament in
the Valley of Pain. She explains her race to them,
a race of mighty rulers once respected of man,
and she points out the plants and the animals of
sorrow ; and towards evening she leads them to
the graves of her ancestors and to the Sibyls and
prophets. At night they come to the presiding
monument, which, like the Sphinx, immortalises
the face of man. When they, but newly dead,
do not fully understand, her gaze releases from
behind the monument an owl, which outlines for
them in its flight the monument's contours. Then
she shows them the new stars of the Land of Pain
and accompanies them to the ravine where they
see the source of the River of Joy, which flows
into the land of man from this country of sorrow.
After parting from her they continue alone and
noiselessly into the ancient Mountains of Pain.
The Elegies end with Rilke's reflection that these

dead, could they convey to us a symbol of happiness from their infinity of death, would point to the empty catkins of the drooping hazel or to the rain which falls, thus rebuking us for believing in a rising tide of fortune.

In this concluding Elegy, which follows immediately upon the vindication of human existence, Rilke fulfils one of his purposes, "das Leben gegen den Tod hin offen zu halten." It was not his purpose to give any complete account of human existence in death. He merely intended to demonstrate the unity of life and death by exhibiting their common principle—suffering—in an allegorical action, in which, moreover, only those are concerned who die young.

Many elements of this allegory cannot be understood except with reference to his most intimate personal experiences. He has explained that the 'landscape of death' became clear to him when he saw Egypt. Such mysterious events as the flight of the owl around the Sphinx are incorporated in the Elegy because they did in fact form part of his actual experience and help him. He has also frequently said that he understood the meaning of death only when he thought of those who had died at an early age, even as he comprehended life only in the figure of the lover. What is true of this

L

Elegy applies to the work as a whole : the composition depends as much on the poet's reminiscences (which remain unexplained) as on the play
of imagination and the elaboration of thought.
From such varied poetic impulses there has
nevertheless resulted an entirely homogeneous
creation.

To many, however, it will seem that Rilke has
left the last word unsaid.   References to the Deity
are singularly infrequent and guarded in a work
that so pre-eminently treats the most fundamental
issues.   It has often been observed that after his
Stunden-Buch Rilke tends to avoid all mention of
God.   But it would be wrong to conclude from
this that therefore he implicitly denies the existence of a Deity.   For his work as a whole, and
the Elegies in particular, God remains ultimately
the centre of his thought, though he is no longer
content to describe Him with the effusive imagery
of the *Stunden-Buch*.   In the Elegies God is the
great anonymous reality, unmentioned because He
is unmentionable.   Rilke's attitude is akin to that
of Goethe in the words of Faust :   " Wer darf ihn
nennen ? "   And he maintained it consciously :

" Ich fing mit den *Dingen* an, die die eigentlichen Ver-
trauten meiner einsamen Kindheit gewesen sind, und
es war schon viel, dass ich es, ohne fremde Hilfe, bis zu

den Tieren gebracht habe. . . . Dann aber tat sich mir
Russland auf und schenkte mir die Brüderlichkeit und
das Dunkel Gottes, in dem allein Gemeinschaft ist. So
nannte ich ihn damals auch, den über mich hereinge-
brochenen Gott, und lebte lange im Vorraum seines
Namens, auf den Knieen. . . . Jetzt würdest Du mich
ihn kaum je nennen hören, es ist eine unbeschreibliche
Diskretion zwischen uns, und wo einmal Nähe war und
Durchdringung, da spannen sich neue Fernen, so wie
im Atom, das die neue Wissenschaft auch als ein Weltall
im Kleinen begreift. Das Fassliche entgeht, ver-
wandelt sich, statt des Besitzes erlernt man den Bezug,
und es entsteht eine Namenlosigkeit, die wieder bei
Gott beginnen muss, um vollkommen und ohne Aus-
rede zu sein. Das Gefühlserlebnis tritt zurück hinter
einer unendlichen Lust zu allem Fühlbaren . . . die
Eigenschaften werden Gott, dem nicht mehr Sagbaren,
abgenommen, fallen zurück an die Schöpfung, an Liebe
und Tod . . . ; es ist vielleicht immer wieder nur das,
was schon an gewissen Stellen im Stundenbuch sich
vollzog, dieser Aufstieg Gottes aus dem atmenden
Herzen, davon sich der Himmel bedeckt, und sein
Niederfall als Regen."

The Elegies reflect this tendency to speak of
man and the world without approaching God
directly. He is now the ineffable and unapproach-
able Divine Being of the Old Testament. In many
respects Rilke's religion approximates more to
the creed of the Old Testament than to that of

the New, and frequently he can accept neither. He is averse to the belief in the need of a divine intermediary and in the dogma of original sin. His desire for an ' open ' life, unhampered by the presence of any ' opposites,' is finally explained only by the necessity for him to move freely towards God, and he could not believe that our life in this world made the path to Him any the more circuitous.   The letter just quoted continues :

" Mehr und mehr kommt das christliche Erlebnis ausser Betracht ; der uralte Gott überwiegt es unendlich.   Die Anschauung, sündig zu sein und des Loskaufs zu bedürfen als Voraussetzung zu Gott, widersteht immer mehr einem Herzen, das die Erde begriffen hat. Nicht die Sündhaftigkeit und der Irrtum im Irdischen, im Gegenteil, seine reine Natur wird zum wesentlichen Bewusstsein, die Sünde ist gewiss der wunderbarste Umweg zu Gott,—aber warum sollten *die* auf Wanderschaft gehen, die ihn nie verlassen haben ?   Die starke innerlich bebende Brücke des Mittlers hat nur Sinn, wo der Abgrund zugegeben wird zwischen Gott und uns —, aber eben dieser Abgrund ist voll vom Dunkel Gottes, und wo ihn einer erfährt, so steige er hinab und heule drin (das ist nötiger, als ihn überschreiten).   Erst zu dem, dem auch der Abgrund ein Wohnort war, kehren die vorausgeschickten Himmel um, und alles tief und innig Hiesige, das die Kirche ans Jenseits veruntreut hat, kommt zurück ; alle Engel entschliessen sich, lobsingend zur Erde."

This conception of man's relation to God explains, too, the figure of the angel as presented in the Elegies. Once again Rilke disclaims all connexion with current Christian notions :

" Der ' Engel ' der Elegien hat nichts mit dem Engel des christlichen Himmels zu tun (eher mit den Engel-gestalten des Islam)."

Certain analogies do exist. The angels, both according to Rilke's conception and in Christian thought, are the perfect and glorious first-created of God. But Rilke's definition of their perfection does not agree with that of the theologians. They are, on a higher plane of existence, what the animals are on a lower—a foil to man, stable and decided beings, re-creative even in their intensest abandonment of feeling. They are an example to man of his ultimate purpose, for his task is accomplished in them ; and because this is so they are a source of terror to man, for man, while occupied with making the world invisible, is yet attached to it :

Denn das Schöne ist nichts
als des Schrecklichen Anfang, den wir noch grade
ertragen,
und wir bewundern es so, weil es gelassen ver-
schmäht,
uns zu zerstören.   Ein jeder Engel ist schrecklich.

Rilke explained these thoughts in a letter to his Polish translator:

"Der Engel der Elegien ist dasjenige Geschöpf, in dem die Verwandlung des Sichtbaren in Unsichtbares, die wir leisten, schon vollzogen erscheint. Für den Engel der Elegien sind alle vergangenen Türme und Paläste existent, *weil* längst unsichtbar, und die noch bestehenden Türme und Brücken unseres Daseins *schon* unsichtbar, obwohl noch (für uns) körperhaft dauernd. Der Engel der Elegien ist dasjenige Wesen, das dafür einsteht, im Unsichtbaren einen höheren Rang der Realität zu erkennen.—Daher ' schrecklich' für uns, weil wir, seine Liebenden und Verwandler, doch noch am Sichtbaren hängen."

For this conception it is hardly possible to find a rational explanation. It is a matter of Rilke's personal belief. In good part also the figure of the angel is a personification of some of his most intimate experiences. His letters show that in his later years he prefers to speak of *the* angel (in the singular), and that this angel is the result of a mythopoetic action. We can see the beginning of this when he says:

"Im Blut . . . kennt sich keiner aus, ich bin immerfort allein mit dem meinen, mir fehlts an dem Gegenstand zwischen ihm und mir. Dass ich jetzt anfinge, mir einen zu schaffen!"

Rilke personifies the aims and the difficulties of his life in this superlative figure, and he then renders account to it for his development and his work. The Elegies contain both conceptions : the conception of the generic and that of the personal angel.

Whereas the *conceptions* themselves, being the effluence of Rilke's innermost beliefs and desires, cannot be explained except in terms of these beliefs and desires, the *place* which the angels occupy in the Elegies admits of a readier explanation. We can understand them when we know Rilke's attitude to God.

Since God is an ineffable Being, man cannot be described (positively or negatively) in terms of His image ; he can be compared only with God's other creatures—the animals and the angels. Because the angels too are created beings, man can approach them openly (though necessarily with caution), while he can only move *towards* God. The presence of the angels in the Elegies is therefore explained if we consider them as the only transcendental figures to whom man can be compared and to whom Rilke can address his justification of human existence.

The Duino Elegies are written on the transcendental plane of the angel. It was a conscious effort on the part of Rilke, for in 1915 he writes :

"Die ' Arbeit nach der Natur ' hat mir das Seiende in so hohem Grade zur *Aufgabe* gemacht, dass mich nur sehr selten noch, wie aus Versehen, ein Ding gewährend und gebend anspricht, ohne die Anforderung in mir gleichwertig und bedeutend hervorgebracht zu sein. Die spanische Landschaft (die letzte, die ich grenzenlos erlebt habe), Toledo, hat diese neue Verfassung zum Äussersten getrieben : indem dort, das äussere Ding selbst : Turm, Berg, Brücke zugleich schon die uner-hörte, unübertreffliche Intensität der inneren Äqui-valente besass, durch die man es hätte darstellen mögen. Erscheinung und Vision kamen gleichsam überall im Gegenstand zusammen, es war in jedem eine ganze Innenwelt herausgestellt, als ob ein Engel, der den Raum umfasst, blind wäre und in sich schaute. Diese, nicht mehr vom Menschen aus, sondern im Engel geschaute Welt, ist vielleicht meine wirkliche Aufgabe, wenigstens kämen in ihr alle meine früheren Versuche zusammen."

This passage can be understood as an applica-tion to himself of the task which Rilke had conceived for man. He projects the world into the angel, where it becomes invisible. At the same time, however, he looks upon it with human eyes, attached to its concrete substanti-ality. The Elegies are therefore also written on a human plane at a guarded distance from the angel.

These distinct yet intimately connected attitudes on the part of the poet largely determine the texture and the style of the Elegies, for his speech seems to come from a region that lies midway between two worlds, one of which is accessible to us, while the other transcends us by far. His verse is at the same time austere and intensely moving, with a musicality which is complete but indeterminable in terms of feet and lines. His language is unusually suggestive and yet ' condensed,' at once boldly neological and profoundly etymological, for he infuses into the most usual words, such as ' Anschein,' ' Bezug,' ' leisten,' ' überstehn,' richly individual notions while revealing their original, hidden and almost forgotten meaning.

"Kein Wort im Gedicht"—he says—"(ich meine hier jedes ' und' oder ' der,' ' die,' ' das') ist *identisch* mit dem gleichlautenden Gebrauchs- und Konversations-Worte ; die reine Gesetzmässigkeit, das grosse Verhältnis, die Konstellationen, die es im Vers oder in künstlerischer Prosa einnimmt, verändert es bis in den Kern seiner Natur, macht es nutzlos, unbrauchbar für den blossen Umgang, unberührbar und bleibend."

His cogent and striking images, especially in the Fifth Elegy, both explain and contain his thought ;

they elucidate thought and yet immediately proceed to assume full and independent reality.

In each of their aspects the Duino Elegies reveal a man who has dwelt in another world and on his return must say what he has learned of human life and destiny. This was the task which Rilke had to accomplish after he had completed *Malte Laurids Brigge*. A year or two before he began the Elegies he wrote in a letter:

"Mir graut ein bisschen, wenn ich an all die Gewaltsamkeit denke, die ich im Malte Laurids durchgesetzt habe, wie ich mit ihm in der konsequenten Verzweiflung bis hinter alles geraten war, bis hinter den Tod gewissermassen, so dass nichts mehr möglich war, nicht einmal das Sterben. Ich glaube, es hats nie einer deutlicher durchgemacht, wie sehr die Kunst gegen die Natur geht, sie ist die leidenschaftlichste Inversion der Welt, der Rückweg aus dem Unendlichen, auf dem einem alle ehrlichen Dinge entgegenkommen, nun sieht man sie in ganzer Gestalt, ihr Gesicht nähert sich, ihre Bewegung gewinnt Einzelheit—: ja, aber wer ist man denn, dass mans darf, dass man diese Richtung geht wider sie alle, diese ewige Umkehr, mit der man sie betrügt, indem man sie glauben lässt, dass man schon irgendwo angekommen war, an irgendeinem Ende, und nun Musse hat, zurückzugehen?"

In *Über naive und sentimentalische Dichtung* Schiller has given a valuable explanation of elegiac poetry

by defining it in terms of the differences between
nature and art and between the ideal and the real.
Compared with this interpretation, the conception
which Rilke had of the scope and the inner meaning of the elegy attained to an even higher degree
of significance.   The differences which he lamented
are less temporal than those stated by Schiller,
and in addition he has made of the elegy an
immensely more representative vehicle of sublime
utterance by including in its scope the transition
from lament to praise.   In German literature only
Hölderlin has written elegies that are equally
moving and profound.

CHRONOLOGICAL TABLE
OF CHIEF WORKS

1899   *Mir zur Feier* published.
        Die Weise von Liebe und Tod des Cornets Otto Rilke
          written.
        Geschichten vom lieben Gott written.
        Das Stunden-Buch, I. Teil, written.

1900   *Vom lieben Gott* published.

1901   *Das Stunden-Buch, II. Teil,* written.
        Das Buch der Bilder finished.

1902   *Das Buch der Bilder* (first edition) published.
        Das Rodin-Buch, I. Teil, written.

1903   *Das Stunden-Buch, III. Teil,* written.
        Das Rodin-Buch, I. Teil, published.

1904   *Die Aufzeichnungen des Malte Laurids Brigge* begun.
        Die Weise von Liebe und Tod des Cornets Otto Rilke
          first published in *Deutsche Arbeit.*

1905   *Das Stunden-Buch* published.

1906   *Die Weise von Liebe und Tod des Cornets Cristoph Rilke*
          (final form) published.
        Das Buch der Bilder (second and enlarged edition)
          published.

1907   *Das Rodin-Buch* (both parts) published.
        Neue Gedichte written and published.

1908   *Der neuen Gedichte andrer Teil* written and published.

1910   *Die Aufzeichnungen des Malte Laurids Brigge* finished
        and published.

1912   The first two *Duineser Elegien* written.
       Das Marien-Leben written.
1913   *Das Marien-Leben* published.
1922   *Die Sonette an Orpheus* written.
       Duineser Elegien finished.
1923   *Duineser Elegien* and *Die Sonette an Orpheus* published.
1934   *Späte Gedichte* published posthumously.

COLLECTIONS OF LETTERS

Briefe und Tagebücher aus der Frühzeit, 1899 bis 1902.	Insel-Verlag, Leipzig,	1931
Briefe aus den Jahren 1902 bis 1906.	*Ibid.*	1930
Briefe aus den Jahren 1906 bis 1907.	*Ibid.*	1932
Briefe aus den Jahren 1907 bis 1914.	*Ibid.*	1933
Briefe aus den Jahren 1914 bis 1921.	*Ibid.*	1937
Briefe an seinen Verleger, 1906 bis 1926.	*Ibid.*	1934
Briefe aus Muzot, 1921 bis 1926.	*Ibid.*	1935
Briefe an einen jungen Dichter.	Insel-Bücherei, Insel-Verlag, Leipzig,	1929
Briefe an eine junge Frau.	Insel-Bücherei, Insel-Verlag, Leipzig,	1931
Briefe über Gott.	Insel-Verlag, Leipzig,	1933
13 Briefe an Oskar Zwintscher.	Gesellschaft der Bücherfreunde, Chemnitz,	1931
Lettres à Rodin. Préface de Georges Grappe.	Emile-Paul, Paris,	1931

BIBLIOGRAPHY OF CHIEF
TRANSLATIONS OF RILKE'S WORKS

ENGLISH

The Tale of the Love and Death of Cornet Christopher Rilke. Trans. by M. D. Herter Norton. W. W. Norton, New York. 1932.

Stories of God. Trans. by Nora Purtscher-Wydenbruck and Herter Norton. Sidgwick & Jackson, London. 1932.

Letters to a Young Poet. Trans. by Herter Norton. W. W. Norton, New York. 1934.

The Notebook of Malte Laurids Brigge. Trans. by John Linton. Hogarth Press, London. 1930.

The Life of the Virgin Mary. Trans. by R. G. L. Barrett. C. Triltsch, Würzburg. 1921.

Poems. Trans. by J. B. Leishman. Hogarth Press, London. 1934.

Requiem, and other Poems. Trans. by J. B. Leishman. Hogarth Press, London. 1935.

Sonnets to Orpheus. Trans. by J. B. Leishman. Hogarth Press, London. 1936.

Elegies from the Castle of Duino. Trans. by E. and V. Sackville-West. Hogarth Press, London. 1931.

FRENCH

Les Cahiers de Malte Laurids Brigge. Trad. par Maurice Betz. Emile-Paul, Paris. 1926.

Histoires du Bon Dieu. Trad. par M. Betz. Emile-Paul, Paris. 1927.

Rodin. Trad. par M. Betz. Emile-Paul, Paris. 1928.

Les Elégies de Duino. Traduites et commentées par J. F. Angelloz. Paul Hartmann, Paris. 1936.

ITALIAN

Opere di Rainer Maria Rilke. A cura di Vincenzo Errante. 5 vols. Editioni Altes, Milan. 1930.

M

SOURCES OF QUOTATIONS

PAGE

26 " meine Arbeit, etc." : *Briefe und Tagebücher, 1899-1902*, p. 10.

27 " Wenn ich, etc." : *Briefe aus Muzot, 1921-26*, p. 15.

27 " Verstehen Sie, etc.": *Briefe und Tagebücher, 1899-1902*, p. 53.

28 "Ich habe, etc.": *Briefe und Tagebücher, 1899-1902*, p. 192.

28 " Es gibt, etc." : *Briefe 1906-07*, p. 117.

29 " Unser kleiner Kreis, etc." : *Briefe 1906-07*, p. 183.

30 " niemand als Sie, etc." : *Briefe 1906-07*, p. 118.

30 " dass ich, etc." : *Briefe aus Muzot, 1921-26*, p. 248.

31 " allein, nur, etc." : *Briefe 1902-06*, pp. 308 f.

32 " Meine Arbeit, etc." : *Briefe 1914-21*, p. 284.

33 " Das Porträt, etc." : *Briefe 1902-06*, pp. 316 f.

34 " Ach, es ist, etc." : *Briefe 1906-07*, pp. 32 f.

36 " das ist die Rückseite, etc." : *Briefe 1907-14*, p. 196.

36 " Dass der arme, etc." : *Briefe 1907-14*, p. 207.

37 "Ich... bin, etc." : *Briefe 1907-14*, p. 48.

38 " endlich, Fürstin, etc." : *Briefe aus Muzot, 1921-26*, pp. 100 f.

39 " Erstaunte euch, etc." : The Second Elegy.

40 " last will and testament ": *cf.* J. R. von Salis, *Rainer Maria Rilkes Schweizer Jahre.* Huber, Frauenfeld, 1936, pp. 176 ff.

43 " links with Novalis ": *cf.* F. Nolte, *Der Todesbegriff bei Rainer Maria Rilke, Hugo von Hofmannsthal und Thomas Mann.* A. Lippl, Heidelberg, 1934.

PAGE

44 "Es würde schwerlich, etc.": Thomas Mann, *Rede und Antwort.* S. Fischer, Berlin, 1922, p. 281.

48 "Russia as the land, etc.": *Briefe und Tagebücher, 1899-1902,* p. 419.

48 "in diesem weiten, etc.": *Briefe 1902-06,* p. 213.

49 "Russland grenzt an Gott": *Geschichten vom lieben Gott* ("Wie der Verrat nach Russland kam").

49 "Jetzt sehe ich, etc.": *Briefe 1906-07,* p. 309.

50 "Ich muss mit, etc.": *Briefe 1906-07,* p. 318.

51 "Meine mit dem, etc.": *Briefe und Tagebücher, 1899-1902,* p. 141.

51 "the cloistered seclusion, etc.": *Briefe 1906-07,* pp. 117 f.

52 "Was mein ist, etc.": *Briefe und Tagebücher, 1899-1902,* p. 147.

57 "Wer den Tod, etc.": *Briefe und Tagebücher, 1899-1902,* p. 418.

58 Georg Simmel: *Rembrandt.* Ein kunstphilosophischer Versuch. Kurt Wolff Verlag, Leipzig, 1917 (3rd to 5th thousand), pp. 89 ff.

61 "The faults, the injustice, etc.": *Briefe und Tagebücher, 1899-1902,* pp. 369 f.

65 "Once, when he was, etc.": *Briefe und Tagebücher, 1899-1902,* pp. 143 f.

68 "das erste grosse Ergriffensein, etc.": *Briefe und Tagebücher, 1899-1902,* p. 367.

68 "Ich habe in den, etc.": *Briefe 1907-14,* p. 57.

69 "Es bestehen, etc.": *Erzählungen aus der Frühzeit,* p. 429.

PAGE

69 " Niemand [kann] auf Ehre, etc." : *Erzählungen aus der Frühzeit*, pp. 429 f.

69 "Ich glaube, etc.": *Erzählungen aus der Frühzeit*, p. 460.

71 Maurice Betz : *Rilke vivant*. Emile-Paul Frères, Paris, 1937, p. 221.

71 " Mich ängstigen, etc." : *Briefe 1902-06*, p. 24.

72 " like a star, etc. " : *Briefe 1902-06*, p. 57.

72 " Paris was a similar, etc." : *Briefe 1902-06*, pp. 97 f.

78 " letter to his Polish translator " : *Briefe aus Muzot, 1921-26*, pp. 319 f.

78 " die Tunnels, etc." : *Briefe 1906-07*, p. 259.

78-9 " Unter London, etc." : *Briefe 1902-06*, p. 213.

79 " Du begreifst, etc." : *Briefe 1907-14*, pp. 172 ff., 180 f., 182 f.

81 " Mir graut, etc." : *Briefe 1907-14*, p. 111. Also, Fürstin Marie von Thurn und Taxis-Hohenlohe, *Erinnerungen an Rainer Maria Rilke*. R. Oldenbourg, Munich-Berlin, 1933, p. 16.

82 " In den Elegien, etc. " : *Briefe aus Muzot, 1921-26*, pp. 332 f. [Rilke's own italics.]

83 " Ich bin ein Ungeschickter, etc." : *Briefe 1902-06*, p. 121.

127 *Wendung: Späte Gedichte*, p. 26. Cf. *Waldteich*, ibid., p. 21.

128 " Irrtum, etc." : From rough notes for a projected essay to be called *Erinnerung an Verhaeren* (unpublished).

PAGE
129   " Ich bin gerade, etc." :   *Briefe 1907-14*, p. 254.

129   " Meine Produktivität, etc." :   *Briefe 1914-21*, p. 381.

130   " Unser effort, etc." :   Letter to Gräfin Sizzo, April 12th, 1923 (unpublished).

131   " Wie ist es, etc." :   *Briefe 1914-21*, p. 86.

131   " against the grain " :   *Briefe 1907-14*, p. 197.

132   *Fünf Gesänge August 1914* :   *Späte Gedichte*, pp. 27 ff.

134   " das Leben gegen den Tod, etc." :   *Briefe aus Muzot, 1921-26*, p. 220.

137   " Wer weiss ob, etc." :   December 21st, 1913 (unpublished).

137   " So wenig, etc." :   November 14th, 1915 (unpublished).

141   " Es wird immer, etc." :   *Briefe 1907-14*, p. 115.

141   " Damals fing, etc." :   *Briefe 1907-14*, p. 219.

141   " Noch für unsere, etc." :   *Briefe aus Muzot, 1921-26*, p. 335.

142   " Der Mann hat, etc." :   *Briefe 1907-14*, p. 179.

146   " Ich habe kein, etc." :   *Briefe 1907-14*, p. 175.

153   " Wer weiss, etc." :   *Briefe 1914-21*, p. 87.

155   " Dass eine Menge, etc." :   *Briefe 1914-21*, p. 177.   Cf. *Briefe 1907-14*, p. 347.

162-4 " Ich fing, etc." and " Mehr und mehr, etc." :   *Briefe aus Muzot, 1921-26*, pp. 185 ff.

165-6 " Der Engel der Elegien, etc." :   *Briefe aus Muzot, 1921-26*, p. 337.

166   " Im Blut, etc." :   *Briefe 1907-14*, p. 213.

PAGE

168   " Die 'Arbeit nach der Natur,' etc." : *Briefe 1914-21*,
          p. 80.

169   " condensed " : *Briefe aus Muzot, 1921-26*, p. 220.

169   " Kein Wort im Gedicht, etc.": Letter to Gräfin Sizzo,
          March 17th, 1922 (unpublished).

170   " Mir graut, etc." : *Briefe 1907-14*, p. 111.

The contributors wish to thank Dr. Carl Sieber and Frau
Ruth Sieber-Rilke for kindness shown to them at the *Rilke-
Archiv* in Weimar.